ASHRAM SCHOOLS IN INDIA

PROBLEMS AND PROSPECTS

By

Dr. B.C. Mishra

M.Phil, Ph.D., DDE, PGDHE (IGNOU)
Senior Lecturer in Education
D.P.I.A.S.E, Berhampur
Dist. Ganjam (Orissa)

&

Dr. Alhadini Dhir

Lecturer
Dept. of Home Science
K.K.S. (Govt.) Women's College
Balasore
(Orissa)

DISCOVERY PUBLISHING HOUSE
NEW DELHI-110002

First Published–2005

ISBN: 81-8356-006-7

Published by:

DISCOVERY PUBLISHING HOUSE

4831/24, Prahlad Street, Ansari Road, Darya Ganj
New Delhi–110 002 (India)
Phone: 23279245, • Fax: 91-11-23253475
e-mail: dphtemp@indiatimes.com

Printed at:

Amit Enterprises, Delhi

Preface

The upliftment of long neglected, distressed and untouchables has been a subject of great concern to the educationists, administrators and social workers. Their progress along with that of others will lead to formation of enlightened, advanced and progressive society. Education is the key to unlock their bound probabilities to make them our true fellow travellers. It acts as a liberator since it empowers them to resist exploitation and oppression. Due to this education has been one of the prime concerns of the government and voluntary agencies with regard to the tribal communities of the country.

Since the tribals did not have a congenial environment for education of children at home, dedicated social workers like Thakkar Bapa devised a system of Ashram schools which provided functional and liberal education to tribals along with free boarding and lodging facilities. The entire concept was based on the ancient tradition of Gurukula in which there was a close interaction between the teacher and the student. The first such school was established in 1922, at the Mirakhedi village in the Panchamahal district in Gujarat for the Bhils. Ashram schools are in general residential and they function within highly structured and systematic framework.

The National Policy on Education, 1986 while strongly advocating equity in education has proposed in the policy itself and its programme of Action, 1992 different strategies to strengthen the educational base of the SCs and STs. One of these measures is to open a good number of Ashram Schools for these categories of children. These schools are enriched with different facilities and incentive programmes for the students. Through these facilities and incentives, it is expected that better performance of these students will be attained. Further, these schools have been set up to bring up the disadvantaged children at par with other category of children. How far have these schools been successful in achieving the goal? The present empirical investigation is a modest attempt to answer the above question.

The work has been completed with the supported and sympathy of scholars and friends. So we cannot fail to extend our thanks to them. Moreover, if our endeavour is of any use in helping to educate the tribal children, it will bring great pleasure to us.

We would like to appreciate the cooperation of all the heads and respondents of the sample schools who gladly provided the data for the successful completion of our field work.

Our thanks are due to Mr. Tilak Wasan, Discovery Publishing House, New Delhi for undertaking the publication of this book.

Berhampur
15th January, 2005

Brundaban Chandra Mishra
Alhadini Dhir

Contents

1

Introduction

BACKGROUND OF THE STUDY

Recent years have witnessed increasing concern with the plight of the socially disadvantaged. They are as a group less successful in school (Liebert *et al.* 1979). Many factors, experimentally established, can be ascribed to such a deplorable situation. Socio-economic status (Wylie, 1963; Havighurst, 1964), self-esteem (Rosenberg, 1965), family structure (Herzog and Lewis, 1971), cognitive development (Bernstein, 1962; Rath, 1972), language (Robinson, 1965) and certain motivational and attitudinal factors (Labov *et al.*, 1968) are mostly responsible for discrepancies in academic performance between socially disadvantaged and socially non-disadvantaged groups. Although schooling for every young child has been the responsibility of the Government, yet most of the socially disadvantaged sections, in spite of all possible efforts, remain away from the target.

The disadvantaged child is a product of poverty or more accurately is caught up in the self-perpetuating cycle of poverty and failure. Intricately involved in this cycle is a host of factors as described above or a few more that play a part in preventing the disadvantaged from achieving better in the school.

The scheduled tribes constitute the most backward group among the weaker sections in India. India has the second largest tribal population constituting about 8 per cent of the total population of the country (1991). They are heterogeneous in socio-cultural and economic life, largely conditioned by ecological settings and ethnic environment. For a long time, the tribal people lived in isolation from the social mainstream, maintaining the cultural identity and transmitting their skills and knowledge through oral traditions from one generation to other.

The upliftment of long neglected, distressed and untouchables has been a subject of great concern to the freedom loving masses due to growing popularity of concepts like nationalism, democracy, secularism, socialism, liberty, equality and fraternity. Their progress along with that of others will lead to formation of enlightened, advanced and healthy Indian. In this context our late Prime Minister Mrs. Indira Gandhi (1971) beautifully remarked:

"It is our duty to see that the backward communities are no more neglected. They are to be made our fellow travellers in our way to progress. Their uplift is a must to make our country strong for disparity is the root of all troubles".

Education is the key to unlock their bound probabilities to make them our true fellow travellers. Emphasizing the need for education for the underdeveloped people Mead (1953) says, "Education is needed in all these areas to cope with and repair their destruction already introduced, and beyond this to make it possible for the people, if they choose, to make their place in the community of nations, and to take advantage of the progress of science and technology in improving their standards of living".

Educational development is also a basic requirement for social and economic development as it helps in removing illiteracy and ignorance, which are fundamental characteristics of Harijans and Tribals (Srivastava *et al.* 1971).

Gill (1965) stated about the importance of education for modernizing societies. To him "an illiterate society is unlikely to be in the fore-front of technological creativity nor for that matter to know-how to use new technologies even if they exist for the taking".

Moreover in developing societies education is considered as a crucial investment as it generates much needed skills and knowledge for economic growth. In this context Rao (1966) says, ".... literacy is a value in itself. In addition there is an economic reason, developmental reason for primary education, for it enables children to acquire literacy and to retain it in adulthood, besides cultivating in them the capacity to acquire skills and develop the right attitude to work and production".

Grigson (1947) argues that we need to introduce among the tribal such a kind of education, which would restore confidence in them and equip them to face boldly and experience the exogenous forces of modernization. To put it exactly in his words; "We have to restore and foster the aboriginal's self-respect by protecting him from loss of land, bond service, debt and oppression, to shield him from malaria, yaws and other sickness, to teach him agriculture and an economic organization suited to his habitat and mentality and to educate him not merely to retain and value his own tribal culture but also to take and hold his due place in the economic, political and cultural life of modern India".

Since independence efforts have been made by the Central and State Governments to spread education through a number of schemes like pre-matric and post-matric scholarships, hostels, non-formal education, book bank, supply of uniforms, stationery, mid-day meals and ashram schools etc.

A BRIEF HISTORY OF ASHRAM SCHOOLS

The concept of Ashram school has been derived from the traditional Indian Gurukulas and the Gandhian philosophy of basic education in which the teacher and the taught live together and have close interaction with the purpose of helping the students in the development of complete personality and in sharpening their capacities.

The educational philosophy of 'Ashram' is based on spiritualism, discipline and yoga.

Thakkar Bapa and Indulal Yagnik came for the relief work in the famine-striken areas of Dohad and Zalod talukas under the instructions of Gandhiji. Thakkar Bapa was moved by the miserable conditions of the tribals and thus decided to devote his life for the uplift of the tribals.

Dohad became the centre of his reform and educational activities. Under the inspiration of Gandhiji, Thakkar Bapa initiated educational activities for the tribal population in western India, presently known as Gjuarat and Maharashtra under the name of 'Ashram schools'. The first Ashram school was started in Mirakhedi, a tribal village in Panchamahal district. Bhill Seva Mandal, a voluntary organization was set up in Panchamahals to coordinate the constructive activities including education of the tribals.

Such Ashrams were also the centres of freedom movement. Their main role was to prepare freedom fighters and social workers. The tribal education work of the Gandhian workers was a part of their broad ideological framework of national liberation. Ashram school was an extension of that logic. After independence the Ashram school retained their existence. However, they had lost their earlier ideological ethos or moral fervour, which was linked with their struggle against the foreign rule (Joshi, 1980).

The Ashram schools, wherever they came into existence, introduced for the first time in that tribal region, a school with residential facility, motivated tribal children for education and created an urge among them to improve their social and moral status. This was no mean achievement.

During the First Five Year Plan there was an attempt by the Government of India to open such schools. However the momentum in opening Ashram schools started increasing from the Third Five Year Plan onwards. The Dhebar Committee (1962) appointed by Government of India suggested establishment of Ashram schools for tribal children particularly in sparsely populated interior backward areas where the normal schools are not available. The number of

Ashram schools in India and enrolment in these schools at three points of time (i.e. 1960-61, 1970-71 and 1980-81) are presented below. (cf. Table 1.1)

The establishment of Ashram school was envisaged as a direct intervention to tackle the socio-economic and geographic inequalities of the tribal population, particularly sparsely populated areas by providing educational opportunities. The concept of Ashram schools stemmed from the objective of providing an atmosphere in which the inmates are offered full opportunities to develop their personality and out-look marked with a high sense of responsibility towards their own community. In addition to formal schooling, these institutions aim at fostering qualities of leadership, communication of new ideas and decision-making ability among the inmates. The main objectives of Ashram schools as envisaged by the various committees and commissions are:

1. To impart general formal education;
2. To encourage tribal traditions like folk songs and dances so that the schools are not only mere learning place but also centres of cultural activities;
3. To reduce the drop-out rate and to improve the retention capacity of the school;
4. To wean the children away from an atmosphere which is generally not conducive for the development of their personality and outlook;
5. To impart socially useful crafts along with general education; and
6. To provide close interaction between the teacher and the taught through the increased individual attention.

The concept of Ashram school combines both functional and literary aspects based education relieving the tribal parent off the burden of feeding, the clothing his school going children besides providing a congenial school environment. Further it is expected to inculcate in the pupils a sense of

Table 1.1: No. of Ashram Schools, Enrolment by States in India in 1960-61, 1970-71, and 1980-81

States	*Percentage of Tribal population to total ST population (1981)*	*1960-61*		*1970-71*		*1980-81*	
		No. of Ashram Schools	*Enrolment*	*No. of Ashram schools*	*Enrolment*	*No. of Ashram schools*	*Enrolment*
Andhra Pradesh	5.93			187	10150	410	30603
Assam				1	210	4	1039
Bihar	8.31					77	10982
Gujarat	14.22	48	3411	135	13451	182	18638
Haryana							
Himachal Pradesh	4.61	7	209	3		7	209
Jammu & Kashmir						1	20
Karnataka	4.91			135	8197	112	7275
Kerala	1.03	14	420	55	1650	55	1650
Madhya Pradesh	22.97			135		187	
Maharashtra	9.19	24	2481	89	8521	300	
Manipur	27.30					6	527
Meghalaya	80.58						
Nagaland	83.99						

Orissa	22.43	59	2851	110	1220	110	1220
Punjab							
Rajasthan	12.21	7	143	6	150	11	500
Sikkim	28.27						
Tamilnadu	1.07	30	1375	73	4264	114	7045
Tripura	28.44						
Uttar Pradesh	0.21			14		12	1220
West Bengal	5.63			1	180	9	937
Total States		189	10890	994	47994	1598	81898
Andaman	11.85						
Arunachal	69.82						
Chandigarh							
Dadra	78.82			71	75	94	744
Delhi				3	242		
Goa	0.99					2	407
Lakshadweep	93.82						
Mizoram	93.55						
Pondicherry							
Total(UTS)				17	317		1151
Total	7.76	189	10890	948	48311	1609	83049

Source: Educational Statistics for Scheduled Castes and Schedule Tribes, 1984, Ministry of Education, Government of India, New Delhi.

service to society and link the school learning with household and community activities.

Consequently, Ashram schools are expected to reduce the incidence of absenteeism, wastage and stagnation and improve the standard of education at primary level. Further it is also intended to reduce the burden on tribal parents by saving them, from incurring expenditure on their children's education as these Ashram Schools provide free board and lodging facilities apart from supplying books, stationery, clothes (uniforms) etc. to the inmates. All these facilities have been provided to favourably motivate the tribal children and their parents towards education.

Ashram schools are in general residential and the inmates are provided with facilities of board and lodging, moreover, they function within highly structured and systematic framework.

The broad policy guidelines for the Ashram schools as envisaged by various committees and study groups on tribal welfare programmes are:

1. Ashram schools should be inter-village schools;
2. Ashram schools should be opened in such areas where normal schools cannot be opened;
3. Most backward tribal groups should be covered.

Generally the Ashram schools provided education up to V standard but in some cases the classes are from I to VII or IV to VII or even I to X. The pattern, size and policy of admission to the institutions differ from state to state. Ashram schools are from only 4 to 5 per cent of the total primary educational system for the tribal population.

Ashram school scheme was originally a centrally sponsored scheme, operated by the states. In spite of this their structure, functioning and objectives widely vary among the states to such an extent that it is difficult to find similarities in their working pattern, or in resource allocation.

In some states such as Gujarat, Maharashtra and Orissa the Ashram schools are of three levels, primary, middle and secondary, whereas in Rajasthan and Andhra Pradesh they only cover the primary level of education. Vocational or craft education strongly envisaged to be implemented in the Ashram schools, has not taken roots, except in a few schools in Maharashtra and Gujarat and Orissa. Mostly the Ashram schools function like general schools with free board and lodging facilities within highly structured and systematic framework. The voluntary organizations, which run Ashram schools in Gujarat and Maharashtra have special problems in fulfilling the conditions, laid by the Government for eligibility to grants. Therefore, appropriate modification in the Grant-in-aid code are necessary enabling Ashram schools to function in such a way as to promote tribal welfare and education.

In Orissa there are four types of schools, which are under the control of Harijan and Tribal Welfare Department having different nomenclatures. They are sevashrams (primary schools), Residential sevashrams (Residential primary schools, Ashram schools and Kanyashrams (Residential middle schools) and High Schools (Residential secondary schools). The number of the different types of schools since the sixth Five-year Plan is given in Table 1.2. The latest position of different types of students on roll in different types of schools that was available to the investigator from the Directorate, Harijan and Tribal Welfare Department, Bhubaneswar is given in Table 1.3.

Besides these schools, a large number of Primary, Middle and Secondary schools are also functioning under the control of Education and Youth Services Department in the state where the students from all sections are on roll.

RATIONALE OF THE STUDY

In pursuance of the directives of the Indian constitution and the special provisions made therein for the STs, the Government of India has been implementing special programmes for the socio-economic development of these

Table 1.2: Number of Different Types of Schools of Harijan and Tribal Welfare Department, Orissa from 1984-85 Onwards

Year	*High Schools*			*Ashram Schools*				
	Boys	*Girls*	*Total*	*Ashram*	*Ashram Kanyashram*	*Total*	*Residential Sevashrams*	*Sevashram*
1984-85	90	27	117	58	9	67	34	1,139
1985-86	90	27	117	58	9	67	34	1,139
1986-87	97	30	127	64	11	75	38	1,121
1987-88	109	30	139	61	18	79	38	1,113
1988-89	117	33	150	62	23	85	50	1,091
1989-90	128	33	161	NA*	NA*	NA*	NA*	NA*

*NA = Not available

Source: Compiled by the investigator from the report of the works of Harijan and Tribal Welfare Department, Government of Orissa. Harijan and Tirbal Welfare Department 1988-89(Oriya version) and data collected through personal contact with the Directorate.

Table 1.3: Different Types of Students on Roll in Different Types of Schools of Harijan and Tribal Welfare Department of Orissa in the Session 1987-88

Type of schools	*SC*	*ST*	*Others*	*Total*
High schools	5,737	18,256	5946	29939
Ashram schools Kanyashram	1,836	4,672	1241	7749
Residential Sevashrams	583	3,290	277	4150
Sevashrams	18,954	49,368	30324	98646

Source: Compiled by the investigator from the Report of the works of Harijan and Tribal Welfare Department, Government of Orissa W.D. through personal contact with the Directorate.

tribal groups. The major objectives of these programmes have been to develop these aboriginals in the direction of modernity so as to enable them to secure for themselves an equitable and rightful place in the national system. But researchers and social workers have expressed their dissatisfaction about the educational progress of the weaker section like SCs and STs. A large amount of money is spent during different five-year plans under the head of special education and educational incentives for Harijan and Tribals. A separate department is working in different states for their social security and welfare. Since 1963-64, the Government of Orissa has opened high schools to provide special scope of higher education to Harijan and Tribal students. These high schools (Ashram type) aim at bringing about a total development of Adivasi Children. With an emphasis on agriculture and other allied handicrafts these high schools intend to train tribal children to become idealistic, service-minded and selfless citizen of the nation (Apte, 1960).

Further, the Government of Orissa is spending a lot of money for these schools expecting the outcomes in terms of objectives for which these schools have been set up. Many scholars have reported the backwardness of the SCs and STs children in general schools in comparison to other caste children. These schools have been set up to bring up the disadvantaged children at par with other category of children. In this context a question arises, "How far these schools are successful to uplift the SC and ST students to the level of other category of students?"

In order to answer the above question a systematic inquiry is highly essential to evaluate these types of schools. Every programme needs its evaluation. The Ashram type of school is a nation-wide experimentation for educational development of the SCs and STs. So the evaluation of these Schools has some implications for the policy makers.

This study will also assist the Government and administrators to get an idea of success of establishing these schools. Accordingly actions can be taken for further plan and programmes.

The teaching personnel and other workers directly or indirectly dealing with the teaching-learning process of these schools will be conscious of their duties. The parents anxious about the development of their wards will get an idea about these schools and may help them to think over the future of their wards career and placement.

The development of a state or nation is interlocked with the development of the backward people. For their accelerated progress the extra amount is being spent from public exchequer. The public will get an idea of the development of the students of those communities placed in the special schools and will verify the justification of spending extra money in comparison to high schools under the Department of Education.

The above urgencies necessitate this type of study, which can explore the extent of responsibilities these schools have been able to shoulder.

STATEMENT OF THE PROBLEM

The researchers have reported that the children of SCs and STs are culturally deprived, socio-economically disadvantaged and educationally backward in relation to the total population of our country. The post independent era witnessed sporadic efforts to bring-up the deprived children to the existing national level through education.

The National policy on Education—1986 while strongly advocating equity in education has proposed in the policy itself and in its programme of Action—1992 various strategies to strengthen the educational base of the scheduled caste and scheduled tribes. One of these measures is to open a good number of Ashram schools for SC and ST children. These schools are enriched with different facilities and incentive programmes for the students. Through these facilities and incentives, it is expected that better performance of these students will be attained.

In this perspective, it is germane to evaluate the role played by the residential schools popularly known as Ashram schools which are established in different states for the SC and ST children with the purpose to cover sparsely populated areas and not to allow the SC and ST students to feel diffident to compete as it happens in the normal schools. The problem therefore, is to what extent these schools have been able to improve the achievement of these deprived children in comparison to Education Department high schools.

ASSUMPTIONS

The following assumptions were made for the study:

1. Different set of facilities have different effects on the education of the students and the set of facilities are comparable.
2. Different socio-economic status of students have different effects on education of the students and the socio-economic status are comparable.
3. Different schooling system (i.e. HTW and Education Department schools) have different effects on achievement of students and the achievement of students are comparable.

OBJECTIVES

The study aimed at achieving the following objectives:

1. To investigate the socio-economic background of the students of Ashram High Schools in comparison to Education Department High Schools.
2. To evaluate the facilities of Ashram High Schools taking Education Department High Schools as parameter.
3. To evaluate the performance of students of Ashram High Schools with reference to students of Education Department High Schools at the Annual H.S.C. examination.
4. To evaluate the attitude, level of occupational and educational aspirations and n-ahv of students of Ashram High Schools taking the students of Education Department High Schools as the parameters.

HYPOTHESES

The null hypotheses formulated for testing in this study are:

1. There will be no significant difference in socio-economic status between the students of Ashram High Schools and Education Department High Schools.
2. There will be no significant difference in the mean scores on different facility areas of Ashram High Schools and Education Department High Schools.
3. There will be no significant differences in the distribution of performance at the Annual H.S.C. examination between:
   (i) the SC/ST students and the non-SC/ST students of Ashram High Schools;
   (ii) the SC/ST students and the non-SC/ST students of Education Department High Schools;
   (iii) the SC/ST students of Ashram High Schools and the SC/ST students of Education Department High Schools;

(iv) the SC/ST students and the non-SC/ST students; and

(v) the students of Ashram High Schools and the students of Education Department High School.

4. There will be no significant differences in mean scores of attitude towards school, teacher, classmates and curriculum between:

   (i) the SC/ST students and the non-SC/ST students of Ashram High Schools;

   (ii) the SC/ST students and the non-SC/ST students of Education Department High Schools;

   (iii) the SC/ST students of Ashram High Schools and the SC/ST students of Education Department High Schools;

   (iv) the SC/ST students and the non-SC/ST students; and

   (v) the students of Ashram High Schools and the students of Education Department High Schools.

5. There will be no significant differences in the distributions of the level of occupational aspiration between:

   (i) the SC/ST students and the non-SC/ST students of Ashram High Schools;

   (ii) the SC/ST students and the non-SC/ST students of Education Department High Schools;

   (iii) the SC/ST students of Ashram High Schools and the SC/ST students of Education Department High Schools;

   (iv) the SC/ST students and the non-SC/ST students; and

(*v*) the students of Ashram High Schools and the students of Education Department High Schools.

6. There will be no significant differences in the distributions of the level of educational aspiration between:

   (*i*) the SC/ST students and the non-SC/ST students of Ashram High Schools;

   (*ii*) the SC/ST students and the non-SC/ST students of Education Department High Schools;

   (*iii*) the SC/ST students of Ashram High Schools and the SC/ST students of Education Department High Schools;

   (*iv*) the SC/ST students and the non-SC/ST students; and

   (*v*) the students of Ashram High Schools and the students of Education Department High Schools.

7. There will be no significant differences in mean scores of achievement motivation between:

   (*i*) the SC/ST students and the non-SC/ST students of Ashram High Schools;

   (*ii*) the SC/ST students and the non-SC/ST students of Education Department High Schools;

   (*iii*) the SC/ST students of Ashram High Schools and the SC/ST students of Education Department High Schools;

   (*iv*) the SC/ST students and the non-SC/ST students; and

   (*v*) the students of Ashram High Schools and the students of Education Department High Schools.

DEFINITION OF THE TERMS USED

The terms used are defined here as under:

Evaluation

Evaluation has been mostly defined in the context of educational programme or curriculum. On this basis, the investigator has defined evaluation in the context of the institution.

Cronbach (1963) described evaluation as the collection and use of information to make decision about an educational programme. The basis of the evaluation is broad personality changes and major objectives of an educational programme (Monroe, 1945). These include not only subject matter achievement, but also attitude, interest, ideals, way of thinking, work habits and personal and social adaptability.

Gayen *et al.* (1970) defined evaluation as an over all estimation of students attainment before and after a course in respect of behavioural changes.

Evaluation designated a process of appraisal which involves the acceptance of specific values and the use of a variety of instrument of observation, including measurement as the basis of value judgements (Ralph, 1951).

Encyclopaedia of Educational Research (Harris ed, 1960) has given an overall picture of evaluation. Evaluation in education signifies describing something in terms of selected attributes and judging the degree of acceptability of that which has been described. The something that is to be described and judged may be any scene, but it is typically (a) a total school programme, (b) curricular procedure, (c) an individual or a group of individuals.

Micheels and Karen (1950) described two steps of evaluation, it attempts to determine what is to be measured, and selecting or developing an instrument that will best do the measuring.

It is apparent from the above discussion that before going to evaluate anything, one should determine at first, what is to be evaluated, secondly 'why' it is to be evaluated, and thirdly, 'how" it is to be evaluated.

Further, it is also concluded that there are three steps in the evaluation process namely, (i) selecting the reliable and valid criterion (ii) selecting the suitable technique, (iii) drawing evidences. Keeping all these facts in view, evaluation for the present purpose is defined as the estimation of overall student progress using different techniques against a suitable criterion.

In the present study the progress of student achievement of Ashram High Schools will be estimated against the process of student achievement of Education Department High Schools.

Ashram High Schools

In the present study Ashram High Schools, having the class up to grade X are those residential high schools, which are managed by the Harijan and Tribal Welfare Department, Government of Orissa. In these schools free lodging and boarding and medical care are provided to the SC and ST students.

Student Achievement

It is the performance of a student in the school subjects. Achievement trends to mean knowledge attained or skills developed in the school subjects usually designated by test scores or by marks assigned by teachers or both. Sawin (1971) says that "achievement is the accomplishment of students, usually the extent to which educational objectives or goals have been attained, that means attainment of student in defined behavioural objectives".

According to Atkins (1958) we may think of achievement as consisting (i) increase in variety of stimulus dimensions to which the learner will be sensitive and responsive, (ii) increase in the number of new responses to be made in novel stimulus situations, (iii) increase in the number of new responses that will be made familiar or already discriminated stimulus components.

In the present investigation, student achievement is defined as the overall attainment of a student to achieve educational objectives of the institution. It refers to acquirement of students in mental and personality field through schooling. The student achievement in the following areas has been measured during the course of research. These are also defined operationally.

(a) *Result of H.S.C. Examination*

It is defined as the performance of the students at the Annual H.S.C. examination conducted by the Board of Secondary Education, Orissa.

(b) *Attitude*

An attitude is often defined as a tendency to react favourably or unfavourably towards a designed class of stimuli. In actual practice, the term attitude has been most frequently associated with social stimuli and with emotionally toned responses.

According to Allport (1954) attitude is a mental and neutral state of readiness, organized through experiences, exerting a directive or dynamic influences upon the individual responses to all objectives and situations with which it is related.

In Dictionary of Education (1959) attitude is defined as "a state of mental readiness to react to situations, persons, or things in a manner of harmony with a habitual pattern of response previously conditioned to or associated with these stimuli".

Attitude is a socio-psychological phenomenon—a human behaviour which is manifested by a good number of people living in a particular group. It differs from individual to individual and from social group to social group.

Attitude is manifested through activities and behaviours. But when it is voiced it is often something else. The expression of the attitude is often influenced by many social, economic and cultural factors.

Although attitude is interpreted through the observation of behaviour, it is very difficult to avoid the subjective biases in such cases. On the other hand, only opinions are susceptible to a quantitative evaluation. To make evaluation based on scientific measurement the fundamental postulates of a continuum and a scale for the placing of the individual must be accepted.

In spite of complexity of the nature of the variable attitude and a wide variation of the different psychologists towards it, we have traced out core of concept and find out the relevance of the different features to the practical task of measurement. For the present study, the attitude is interpreted to mean varying degree of 'liking' and 'disliking of individual to different areas, objectives, ideas, programmes etc. which is manifested in variable reaction; varying degrees of which are inferred from the scale.

(c) Aspirations

An individual's aspirations are his expectations, goals or claims in a dynamic situation on his own future achievement in a given task in regard to the goodness of his own future. The expectations which are merely imaginative, fantastic, unrealistic, below or above one's self-esteem is called idealistic level of aspiration and where ones actual performance and expectations are about the same it is called realistic level of aspiration. Aspiration is a psychological variable having motivational role and can cause satisfaction or frustration depending upon the result of success of failure in achieving the goal.

I. Occupational Aspiration

The concept of level of occupational aspiration logically originated from the special instance of the concept of level of aspiration. Level of aspiration is a psychological construct which reflects a cognitive type of motivation of the individual.

In the present study occupational aspiration is an individual's expectation or ambition for near or distant future which refers to his estimate of his performance in the occupational prestige hierarchy. This is a socio-psychological variable which takes its occupational prestige hierarchical form from the social structure. It motivates the individual to try his best for its accomplishment. For the present purpose occupational aspiration connotes the aspiration as measured by occupational aspiration scale prepared by Grewal (1984).

II. Educational Aspiration

It is a psycho-social construct which reflects a cognitive type of motivation of an individual. It involves the estimation of an individual's ability for his future performance in the educational hierarchy on the strength of his past performance, his capacities and the efforts that he can make towards attaining the goal, thus set by him.

Educational Aspiration in the present study refers to the total score of the individual on the Educational Aspiration scale of Sharma and Gupta (1980)

(d) Achievement Motivation

The term achievement motivation was first introduced by Mcclelland (1953). He said that achievement motivation can be designated as a need or desire to excel in a wide variety of situations. When the motive is aroused, it is expressed in driving energy directed towards attaining excellence, getting ahead, improving our pervious work, doing things better, faster which require ingenuity and persistence. People with high achievement motive generally are self-confident individuals who function best in situations where they assume personal responsibilities and can control what happened to them.

The formulation of achievement motive, otherwise known as need achievement (n-Ach), construct derives primarily from the work and theory of Murray (1938). Achievement motive has been reported to as the need for achievement since the beginning of its systematic study (Mcclelland *et al.* 1949).

Achievement motive is defined as a disposition to strive for success or the capacity to experience pleasure contingent upon success (Atkinson, 1957). It involves a concern for competition with some standard of excellence.

Achievement motive has been conceptualized as individual's orientation to endeavour for conduction of activities in those situations where the performance has to be evaluated. As a motive force it functions in the form of a relative stable characteristic of personality after the period of early socialization during which it develops (Atkinson, 1958).

The n-Ach is a pattern of planning up action and of feeling connected with striving to achieve some internalized standard of excellence. Achievement motivation is not necessarily the same thing as the search for observable accomplishment.

Achievement motivation is a set of learned motives to complete and to strive for success. Because almost all activities can be viewed in terms of competition and success vs. failure, the need to achieve influences behaviour in a large number of quite diverse situations and because it is a learned motive, there are wide differences among individuals in their past experiences and hence in their motivation with respect to achievement. There is a universal tendency in man to strive, to excel and succeed and to win and go ahead of others.

For the purpose of this study achievement motivation may be defined as dissatisfaction with the present condition and an urge to improve upon the same condition of life (Mehta, 1967).

(e) Socio-economic Status

The term socio-economic status is a complex one to define due to complexity in class status and power. Due to the difficulty in defining the term, many scholars in the field defined the term on the basis of the contributing variables.

Green (1975) defined socio-economic status as "a position in a social group or grouping in relation to other positions held by other individuals in the same group or grouping".

Broucke (1975) has used socio-economic status in a broad sense so as to include education, profession and economic status of parents. Some environment accessories are also taken into consideration. In India social status generally includes educational and professional status, i.e. the term has been taken to mean both education and occupational status.

Havinghurst and Neugarten (1954) have identified the following factors determining the social status of a persons: (a) Occupation, (b) House type, (c) Area lived in, (d) Source of income, (e) Amount of income, and (f) Amount of education.

Kupuswamy (1962) has defined the term 'SES' in relation to social prestige. He states that education, occupation and income is the composition of social status. For Pareek and Trivedi (1964) socio-economic status refers to composition of variables like caste, occupation, education, social participation, land, house, farm, power material possession and type of family.

The investigator after reviewing the above definitions and consulting the experts in the field framed the following as an operational definition. The definition states "the socio-economic status of a person is determined by the state of the person in (a) education (b) occupation, (c) income (d) land (e) type of social participation (f) type of house owned (g) material possession in relation to other contemporaries" (Kamila, 1985).

(f) Facility

Every school has its own facilities to facilitate learning teaching process. These facilities generally include school building rooms, playground, kitchen, garden, teaching materials, furniture and economic resources. The economic resources consist of salaries, stipend, contingency grants etc. These facilities may be broadly of three types, i.e. physical facilities, material facilities, and economic facilities.

For the present purpose the facilities of a school is defined as the existing physical material and economic provisions under the possession of the school used for the learning teaching purpose.

DELIMITATIONS OF THE STUDY

Following are the delimitations of the present study:

1. The present study is confined to evaluation of Ashram High Schools in respect of student achievement, keeping in mind the student's socio-economic background and facilities of these high schools.
2. Through schooling the students can develop in various aspects viz physical, social, scholastic and in area related to personality, attitude, interests, intelligence, aspirations, aesthetic and moral etc. But the present study has been delimited to the following areas to student achievement: attitude, occupational and educational aspirations, and achievement motivation.
3. The study has been conducted on X graders. The sample was drawn only from six districts of Orissa, namely Balasore, Keonjhar, Cuttack, Dhenkanal, Ganjam and Phulbani.
4. The statistical techniques like t-test, chi-square and percentage analysis were employed.

2

REVIEW OF RELATED LITERATURE

It is worth while for a researcher to make a comprehensive survey of what has already been done on the problem and its related aspects. Mouly (1964), therefore, states, "survey of related literature avoids the risk of duplication, provides theories, ideas, explanations or hypotheses valuable in formulating the problem and contributes to the general scholarship of the investigator".

Practically all human knowledge can be found in books and libraries. Unlike other animals that must start with each generation, man builds upon the accumulated and recorded knowledge of the past (Best, 1959).

The importance of related studies can not be denied in any research because it is an important aspect of the research project. In this context, Goode, Barr and Scates (1941) have aptly remarked, "The competent physician must keep abreast of the latest discoveries in the field of medicine. Obviously, the careful student of education, the research worker and the investigator should become familiar with the location and use of sources of educational information".

It is evident from the above discussion that for any worth while investigation, a review of related literature in the field of investigation is off great help to the researcher. The studies tell us how much work has already been done in a certain field and provide necessary knowledge and insight about the methods used to collect, analyses and interpret data and findings. It also suggests solutions and recommendations.

It provides clear path to the researcher. It helps the researcher to discover the facts which had remained unexplored in the previous studies. In the present study an attempt was made to go through the literature concerned with investigation in hand as well as reference books, monographs, Government publications on Education, Encyclopaedia of Education, research conducted in the field of tribal education, educational abstracts and journals etc. In this chapter, the researcher has presented some related studies concerning the tribal education, education of the disadvantaged and Ashram Schools in India and abroad.

STUDIES ABROAD

The investigator has gone through a large number of studies on the culturally deprived and disadvantaged children. Studies having direct bearing upon the present work are conspicuous by their absence. However, some of the significant studies, which have direct or indirect bearing upon the study in hand, have been presented below.

Davis (1948) states that the physically and socially aroused anxiety of lower class people derive from the uncertainty of having food, fear of eviction, fear of being cold in dark. Therefore, whenever they have food they eat too much and whenever they have money, they spend too much to reduce anxiety and protect themselves against the uncertain future.

Korchhoff (1959) in his studies following the work of MC Clelland, collected TAT stories from 63 Chippewa Indian children stories and 76 white children. All were students in the fifth through tenth grade in school. The result indicates that whites express more achievement motivation than the Indians. Within the Indian group those with mixed or ambivalent group identifications indicate the least achievement motivation than younger children.

Leshan (1952) reports that disintegrated children are more present oriented and they have vague and indefinite notions about the future and little sense of pattern and regularity. This finding seem to be consistent with those of Henderson (1966) who found that low potential families were more concerned with meeting their daily needs than providing experiences, that would have future educational pay-off. Lack of sense of pattern and regularity may arise out of temporal and spatial disorganisation in their disadvantaged homes". Most disadvantaged do not have a regular meal time can be taken to represent "the most basic ordering event by which one can begin to develop time concepts and a future orientation (Miller, 1968). These personal style variables are the real psychological processes operating in them which keep them away from sharing the experiences and information with more advanced sections of the society. Those basic psychodynamic aspects of these groups of persons should be properly handled by the well-intentioned psychologists and educationists who should have special training for treating the cognitive deficits.

Kohn (1959) has studied "social class and parental values". According to him, social class in a reliable indicator of values. Parents of fifth grade children coming from middle class and working class families were interviewed. Both the groups of parents agreed on the importance of honesty, consideration, obedience, and dependability for boys and girls. Middle class parents emphasized self-control and dependability in their children while working class parents place greater value on neatness, cleanliness and obedience to externally imposed standards.

Rosen and D' Andrrode (1959) have documented the dependence of achievement motivation upon certain parental variables. Parents of high need achievement boys were interacting more with their children. The stressed independence and self-reliance on the part of their children by giving hints to solve problem than doing the problem for them. Farley and Hermalin (1972) demonstrated that the racial gap in education, occupational achievement and income narrows during the 1960s. While citing some important exception and nothing that in many access the racial disparities remain quite large, the authors suggest that progress towards racial equality was made in the decade from (1960 to 1970).

Feld Husen and Klausmeir (1962) find that SES is related with anxiety, educational aspiration and self concept. Positive attributes are more closely associated with high SES than with low SES. There exists a positive relationship between SES and anxiety for low SES children. All the more, when these low SES children are taught in schools, their failure experiences begin to eradicate emotionally erosive effects. Thus they become anxious and maintain pessimistic expectations for educational, and occupational success and success in life in general.

Other researches include: A study by Reissman (1962) on "The Culturally Deprived Child", Passow, Goldberg and Tannenbaums (1967) study on "Education of the Disadvantaged", Witty's (1967) study on "The Educationally Retarded and Disadvantaged" and Thampsons (1962) on "Problems in Achievement of Adequate Educational Opportunities". These studies have most concentrated on the educational problems of the children of poor sections of the society living in the urban slums of the United States of America. These have reveled that low social-economic status, lack of motivation, olienation from the school and the family, language difficulties in learning process and other factors are the important variables for educational retardation and the early drop-out of children coming from the disadvantaged groups in a society. These studies however, do not have much direct relevance for the understanding of educational problems of the tribal students especially in the Indian settings.

Strauss (1962) has characterized affluent society as the achievement oriented society. His findings suggest a good degree of relationship of deferred gratification and need achievement, to social class. Hence members from high social class provide evidence of a high degree of motivation which accounts party for their success in educational and occupational world.

Jones (1963) maintains that lower class individuals do not consider education as a means for upward mobility not because they devalue education but they do not expect to rise too far in the occupational world. All the more achievement in school is not accompanied by their basic needs. Since they prefer to work under concrete rewards over more abstract reinforcements in learning tasks (Tarrel, Durkin and Wiesley, (1959), high rate of stagnation and drop-out cases is not astonishing. They have a preference of immediate reinforcement of delayed reinforcement when they are assured of greater rewards and delayed conditions Kahl, 1965, Maitland 1966, Skin 1966). Where authors have shown that "the ability to delay gratification in related to SES, is higher intellectual functioning and such family variables as fathers presence or absence and conditions of family disorganization".

Deutsch (1964) remarks that disadvantaged children being raised in noisy environment with little organized and sustained conversation fail to distinguish and recognize the speech sounds. Thus their auditory learning is greatly retarded during the years conducive to development of linguistic competence. All persuasive verbal under development under development is one of the important reasons as to why they do not profit out of class room instruction.

John and Goldstein (1964) report that low socio-economic status children have more trouble with action words as they have no adequate experience in fitting labels to various forms of actions they have observed. These view points are much in line with those of Bernstein (1965) who interprets his findings as indicative of the difference in the language codes used by the middle and lower class people. He suggest that lower class children use restricted language code pattern mainly characterized by short, simple and unfinished sentences, simple and repetitive use of conjunctions, little use of subordinate clauses, rigid and limited use of adjectives and verbs and too many repetitions of the same word. Restricted language code pattern functionally retains their group integrity and status by excluding non-group members from sharing in the in-group communication. However this also restricts the ability of the lower class people to communicate effectively with outside groups and to receive any information from them for practical use. On the other hand, the middle class is capable for the use of elaborated language code. The language code pattern used by the middle class people is characterized by accurate grammatical and syntactical order, frequent use of prepositions and logical modifications, discriminative selection of adjectives verbs, expressive symbolism and explicit exposition. Linguistic inefficiency is all the more related with low level of conceptualization and linguistic precision. Therefore, learning of the lower class children in school situation on tasks presupposing linguistic proficiency is greatly hampered.

For Deutsch (1965) cumulative deficit phenomenon was responsible for making one drop-out. Such deficits in class-I become more marked in the higher classes. There in a great deal of experimental evidence to show that developmental process before the age of 5 and 6 are extremely important for proper cognitive growth (Bloom *et al.*, 1965).

Green and Farquhas (1965) indicate that SES more than the activity or I:Q correlates highly with expectations for occupation and education. For Negro children the motivational scale predicts their achievement in high school more than the test of intelligence. They have used the motivational scale constructed at the Michigan State University. They have found that the self-concept test, which is one part of the scale predicts the achievement of these Negro children better than other tests. It is found that inferior SES is accompanied by poor school achievement, poor motivation but not necessarily with impaired learning abilities.

Such achievement is also well related with the personality dimension, which Kagan (1965) calls impulsivity reflectivity. Reflectivity returns to the individuals tendency to think over the problem and to consider alternative problem solutions and to delay the response with a view to getting the answer on the other hand, children with impulsive or fast tempos try to solve a problem with little or no delay and ultimately make impulsive and unconsidered responses. The reflective response tendency is related to higher reading achievement, social class and intellectual ability (Kagan 1965, Miller & Mumbauer, 1967). Lack of reflective response in well related to their failure in academic pursuits. Their ability in advanced learning situation is greatly retarded.

Coleman's (1966) study clearly indicates that the differential effects of schools on students are due to largely to the factors existing outside the school. The report of the U.S. Commission on Civil Rights reveals that inequality in public schools on educational attainments along with social class and racial lines. Both these reports indicate that minority group students and those who come from poor social economic families scored significantly lower than their white middle class counterparts.

Disadvantaged children have been shown to manifest significantly lowered self esteem as compared to disadvantaged group. (Long and Hennderson, Le 67; Coleman 1966). Their lowered self-esteem may well be viewed as a manifestation of source of lack of control over the environment. The feeling of inadequacy is related to their failure experience in school related task (Battle and Rotter, 1963). Therefore they lack persistence in school related tasks and poor achievers among the disadvantaged group give higher evaluate rating for school subjects in which they are achieving poorly. (Greenberg, Gerver Chall and Davidson 1965). They also appear to be less sensitive to their or failure experiences in school related task than the middle class children.

Uzgiris (1968) argued that retardation in sensori motor skills is a result of chaotic over stimulation rather than of deficiency in stimulation. The culturally deprived home is characterized by a conflicting array of stimulation with the result that the child is unable to attend these stimuli most relevant in terms of increased intellectually development (Gray and Klaus, 1965). Stimulation in the culturally deprived environmental condition appears to occur within a restricted range and there is less adequate and systematic ordering of stimulation sequences (Deutsch, 1963).

Some significant studies on "Poverty and Children" are reviewed by Bruner (1975). He observed "Persistent poverty over generations creates a culture of survival. Goals are short ranged and restricted. The outsiders and the outside are suspect. One stays inside and gets what one can the issue in to make it possible for the poor to gain a sense of their own power".

Farely (1977) reported that the trend towards equality which marked the prosperous 1960s has not attended as a result of the economic adversity of the early 1970s. Haywood (1967) has hypothesized the existence of more hygiene-oriented individuals among the culturally disadvantaged groups. He argues that "Motivation oriented individuals have been shown to be more persistent in task, learn discrimination reversal problems learn quickly when relevant factors are held constant and perform better on standardized achievements". When motivational and aspirational level of the disadvantaged leads to lack of involvement and persistence in the school relation tasks. Since the class room instructions in educational institutions do not hold to them, the promise of satisfaction of their oft-recurring needs and problems. So, it is not astonising to keep themselves away from the school.

STUDIES IN INDIA

Attempts have been made by the Indian social scientists, educators, psychologists and administrators to study the multidimensional problems of tribal education. Most of the research studies have been conducted on the educational problems of tribals. Some of the studies have been concentrated on the educational backwardness of Harijans and Tribals. Very few studies were conducted in India on variables leading to performance deficit on Tribal and Harijan students. Some of the significant studies have been reviewed below.

Tribal education has suffered from academic and administrative problems too. Studies conducted by Dasgupta (1963), Sachidananda (1967), Srivastav (1970b), Medhi (1980) and Sharma (1983) have shown that the uncongenial home environment does not suit the children in pursuing studies. In this study on identification of educational problems of the Saoras (a tribe), Srivastav (1970b) found that the Saora needed upper primary, middle and high schools in comparison to the lower primary schools, because the progress of primary education was hindered by administrative problems such as school buildings, school management, trained teachers, training materials, staff quarters and proper inspection of schools. The major hindrance being geographical barriers and inaccessibility of tribal village, poor quality of teaching problems of medium of instructions, irrelevant curriculum and text book, more numbers of single teacher schools, uneven teachers students ratio have resulted in high drop-out rate, wastage and stagnation and ultimately resulted in slow growth of tribal education as reported by Ambasht (1966), Srivastav (1970b), Tappo; (1974), Medhi (1980), Sujatha (1980), Sharma (1983) and Kundu (1984).

Notwithstanding the socio-economic, academic and administrative problems in tribal education, the studies have also highlighted some psychological problems too. In this connection Metha (1976) and Sharma (1983) observed that "failure" more than once experienced by the tribal children in the school resulted into a strong sense of insecurity, which is passed onto the young children. Similarly lack of interest, motivation, aspiration and ambition in life and low level intelligence among tribal children were the major impediments found to be coming in their way of education. Ambasht (1966); Sachchidananda (1967); Srivastav (1970b, 1981); Sujatha (1980); Tappo (1974). In this study on problems of early schooling of tribal children, Srivastav (1981) observed that unproductive and traditional type of educational system for tribals was the cause of indifferent attitude of tribal parents towards the education of their children. Another study by Dasgupta (1963) in this regard enlists several reasons for their indifferent attitude, which are: (i) existing system of education was not adjusted to their immediate needs and interests, (ii) they were suspicious of the sincerity of the non-tribal people, who are generally organized and run the educational institutions intended for them, (iii) the system of education took no notice of their indigenous system of training of skills and interests which they already possessed and (iv) there was an acute dearth of tribal teachers who could handle properly the tribal children. With regard to the attitude of the teachers towards students, Sharma (1983) and Kund (1984) have found that non-tribal teachers had negative attitude towards tribal children, and the studies of Ambasht (1966) and Tappo (1974) have shown that tribal children were linking tribal teachers only. Thus it can be concluded that an unhealthy trend of attitude among tribal parents, teachers and students was observed by researchers who conducted these studies. The study of Sharma (1991) highlighted that the educational aspiration of tribal students was lower than the non-tribal students, but their occupational aspiration was higher. For their low self-concept they could not develop confidence according to their capabilities. Similarly Mishra (1996) reported that the phenomenon of tribal drop-out was significantly related to their academic motivation and inferiority complex in hilly area were as in plain area school adjustment was responsible for the school drop-out.

However, in the following pages the researcher has presented the studies in detail.

Aiyappan (1948) has examined the present status of education with special reference to tribal education. His suggestions pertain to the tribal school, vocationally-based education and incentives for the literacy programme for the youth. Apte (1960) has studied the problems of tribal schools in general and of the Ashram schools in particular. Ashram schools according to him, prove to be effective media of social transformation. Banerjee (1962) has tested his two main hypotheses: (1) Medium of instruction in the determinant factor of primary education among the students and it hampers the progress of education of some tribal communities because this aspect has been overlooked in the past; (2) Geographical factor is not a barrier to the progress of primary education among the tribals. Bapat (1961) gives his experience gained as a teacher and points out the shortcomings in the educational system. He suggests that ignorance, which is prevalent among the tribals, should be fought with a well-planned system of education in tribal education. Girl's education should get priority.

Dave (1954) has given a detailed account of Ashram schools and Sevashrams Training Centres in Orissa. The general routine of the Ashram schools has been given along with staff and their pay scales. The details of stipends and scholarships, which the residents get, have also been given. He has discussed literacy among the Grasias. He has also proposed a scheme for education and has suggested to impart industrial and social education.

Patnaik's (1957) appraisal report deals with the curriculum used in the Ashram schools existing in Orissa. The relative importance of different subjects that are taught in Ashram schools has been measured by way of taking proportion of school-time spent on each subject into consideration.

Basu (1958, 1961, 1963) has outlined the type of education to be given to tribesmen and the importance of mother-tongue as medium of instruction. He points out that education, through tribal dormitories, was successfully imparted to the tribal children in the past. Biswas (1955) suggested vocational bias in tribal education. Adult education programmes should be launched in tribal areas on at large scale. Brahma (1953) has dealt with the working of the different types of systems in a Ashram. Reservation of seats in colleges, schools, and in technical schools have been suggested. Dasgupta (1964) has discussed in detail tribal economy with reference to education. Elwin (1959) has suggested that school should become as much a tribal institution as "Morung" (dormitory). In his book titled, "A New Deal for Tribal India" (1963) Elwin has devoted his attention to the educational developments of the tribals. He has discussed education and economics of the tribal school programmes, school buildings, types of schools, equipment and learning environment, medium of instruction, types of teachers and compulsory primary education, technical education, education for tribal girls and dissemination of information about scholarship and other facilities.

Sachchidananda (1958, 1964) has concluded that there in low literacy rate among the tribals. In his articles titled 'Tribal Welfare of Bihar' he has described the problems of tribal education, the duration of the school and the school session, medium of instruction and the type of text books used. Opening of hostels for the tribal should be an important item in the programme for the educational uplift of the scheduled tribes. In his articles (1964) titled "Dhumkuria, Then and Now", he points that Dhumkuria served as an educational institution. In another book, "Culture change in tribal Bihar, Munda and Oran". He has pointed out that education has been one of the major achievements of the Christian Missionaries. Education has not only resulted in literacy but has also served as a means of enlightenment in all aspects of life.

Vyas (1958) has presented a detailed account of ten-year progress of ashram school education in Orissa from 1947-48 to 1957-58. It contains the history of Ashram schools and the present state of affairs. Another study has stressed certain aspects of Ashram schools which he described essential for a good Ashram school i.e. proper utilization of funds, purity atmosphere, honesty and integrity of the school staff and the like.

Apte (1960) has first discussed the tribal problems in general and then the Ashram school and calls the latter a more effective weapon and instrument for social transformation. He has laid down objectives and programme of ashrams and enumerated extracurricular activities. The article contains a tabular analysis of tribal children in Talwada Ashram School.

The study of tribal education and Santals of Dasgupta (1963) reveals the following difficulties faced by their parents in sending the children to schools: (i) lack of cooperation and real contact between parents and schools, (ii) apathetic or indifferent attitude of the parents towards education of their children. Further he gives a list of several reasons for their indifferent attitude, which covers (i) the present system of education is not adjusted to their immediate needs and interests, (ii) they are suspicious of the sincerity of the non-tribal people who generally organize and run the educational institutions intended for them, (iii) the present system of education takes no notice of their indigenous system of training of the skill and interest which they already possess, and (iv) there is an acute dearth of tribal teachers who can handle properly the children.

Mohan (1963) has discussed the activities of residential schools including school buildings, its management, caste-wise, and year-wise enrolment of the students, examination results and other aspects of the school life including sports, life in hostel, daily routine and cultural programmes.

Bose (1963) in his doctoral research work Socio-Psychological study of the Adolescent Tribal children of West Bengal studied the curriculum for the purpose of national integration. Chattopadhyaya (1963) compared the IQ of Tribal and Non-tribal school going boys. Chitnis (1973) studied the status of scheduled caste and scheduled tribe students in the institutions of learning and identified the difficulties and problems faced by them. Desai (1974) in his study, "A Profile of Education Among the Scheduled Tribes in Gujarat" investigated the literacy rate in Gujarat State. He discussed the change in enrolment and utilization of hostel and scholarship facilities. Dubey (1974) studied the scheduled tribe students and how their education affected their aspirations and performance, their way of life and their participation in other activities. George (1975) evaluated the government policies for the education of scheduled castes and scheduled tribe students. Parvathamma (1974) studied the socio-economic background of scheduled caste and scheduled tribe students in order to know its effect on their performance in schools. Their feeling of social alienation, their opinion about governmental facilities and their education aspirations were also studied. Shah and Thakkar (1974) made a study of scheduled caste and scheduled tribe students in order to see how their education has affected the aspiration and performance in terms of life style, participation in co-curricular activities, social outlook, attitudes towards the government facilities and concessions and outlook about the status of scheduled caste and scheduled tribes.

Many more studies have appeared in literature after 1966. Ambasht (1970) in his publication, "A Critical Study of Tribal Education" points out that formal education has changed the attitude of people towards the tribal way of life, social and tribal culture. Shrivatava (1967) in his publication, "Education for the Tribal" and "Applied Anthropology in India" pleads for the provision of facilities to the tribal people for their rapid educational development. He discusses all aspects of education for tribal children including curricula, method of teaching and the medium of instruction. The NCERT Report of the National Seminar held in September. 1965 on "Tribal Education in India" published in 1967 is significant. Kaul (1967) in his article "Existing Facilities, Coverage, Wastage, Stagnation and Utilizaiton of Financial Assistance in Respect of Tribal Education" deals with a wide variety of problems. Sachchidananda (1967) analyses the socio-economic aspects of tribal education. Mahapatra (1967) touches upon the issues of curricula, methodology and text books for the tribal students. Burman (1967) described the role of Government and voluntary agencies in educating the tribal people. Publications like "A Study of the Tribal People" and "Tribal Areas of Madhya Pradesh" have been brought out by Dube and Bahadur (1966). Programmes of the tribal education at different school levels expansion of educational facilities have been highlighted in this publication. The research by Chattopadhyaya on the intelligence of tribal and non-tribal children of Tripura reveals that the tribal group does not compare favourably as a group with the non-tribal boys. Another significant study on the Bhils was conducted by Naik (1969). He analyzed the impact of education on the life of Bhils. He found out that education has considerably affected the cultural life of the tribals of Madhya Pradesh, especially those of the Bhils.

Srivastava et al (1971b) has enlisted a score of educational needs of the tribal people. They includes (i) stipends, (ii) food, (iii) some job for children which can get them some cash and (iv) necessity of children's presence at home to look after the household.

Gokulanathan (1972) studied the achievement related motivation (n-Ach and anxiety) and educational achievement among higher secondary school tribal and non-tribal students. Using stratified random sampling, 294 boys and 89 girls were drawn from secondary schools in three districts of Assam. The tribes included in the study were Kachari, Miri, and Meeh tribes of the early Mongoloid race. The non tribals were mostly non-Mongoloids or Vans of Hindu religion. T.A.T. and Mehta's Achievement value and Anxiety Inventory were used to assess achievement motivation and anxiety. Performance at the SSLC/HSLC examinations and tests served as the index of educational achievement. The study revealed that (i) the tribal students obtained significantly higher n-Ach scores than the non-tribals; (ii) The non-tribals in the rural sample showed significantly greater n-Ach than their tribal counterparts; (iii) the tribal and non-tribal boys in the rural sample do not show significant differences in their n-Ach, but their urban counterparts show a significant difference. The study showed that the tribal boys, irrespective of the area of their residence, have higher level of n-Ach than non-tribal boys.

Rath (1972) reported that the home conditions of the large majority of poor children are not congenial to their adequate cognitive development in their early formative years. In the absence of adequate cognitive and motivational development at home and in the absence of early pre-school educational experience we can understand the fate of such children in class I in the school. The poor children are not able to cope with some of the intellectual tasks needed for this stage of education. These systematic variables interact with each other and become problems for the poor people to pursue their education.

Sachchidananda (1973) conducted a study on socio-economic aspect of tribal education. In this study he reiterated that there was a major link between education and economy. According to him, education could increase the human efficiency which ultimately turned into production. After independence the urgent need for bettering the living condition of the tribal people was realized by the government and large sum of money was allocated for the development programmes of the tribal. Firstly, there was a big controversy among the social workers regarding the relative importance of educational and economic development. It was urged by them that once they were educated they would themselves improve their economic conditions. But after different surveys, it was accepted by all the sections of the people that for the educational development of tribals, it was necessary to improve their economic condition. It was found that tribal parents did not send their children to schools because they helped them increasing their family income.

Similarly findings were reported by Srivastava *et al.*, (1971a). They found that many tribes experienced inadequacy of financial assistance, in some cases the assistance was given to the undeserving, in others assistance was not utilized for the purposes for which it was given and in the rest, the assistance was inadequate at the secondary stage.

The proceedings of the workshop held at the National Institute of Community Development has touched upon various aspects of tribal children. The two articles on tribal education are important including "Education and

Employment Policy Towards Scheduled Tribe in India" (Rao, 1974), and Planning for Educational Facilities in Tribal Areas (Thaha, 1974). A case history of Bastar District of Madhya Pradesh has been presented by Thaha. Apart from taking up various issues related to the education of tribal children, the author has also proposed educational programmes for the Bastar District. Rajagopalan (1974) in his study titled "Educational Progress and Problems of Scheduled Caste and Scheduled Tribe Students in Karnataka" concludes that scheduled tribe students are more liberal in their attitude towards marriage and friendship pattern than scheduled caste students.

Sachchidananda in the his investigation, "Education Among the Scheduled Castes and Schedule Tribes in Bastar", finds inadequacy of physical facilities in schools. He has also dealt with the educational aspirations of the students and attitude of the teachers towards them. Rathnaiah (1977) in his research "Structural Constraints in Tribal Education", has studied the impact of education on the tribal children. Kakra (1967) in his study, "Impact of Education on the Tribal of Ranchi District concludes that intelligent students pickup jobs. The less intelligent ones become delinquents and the educated youth go towards cities. They are neglecting the tribal occupations of agriculture and handicrafts.

The study conducted by Rajagopalan (1974) on the educational progress and problems of SC and ST students in Karnataka reveals that economic condition of the SC/ST students was not sound and involvement in domestic work seemed work to be coming in their way of education. Another study by Desai and Pandor (1974) also reveals that majority of SC/ST students belonged to the low or average economic status. Similarly the study of Joshi (1980) on the educational problems of SC and ST students reveals that 95 SC and ST parents were small farmers or landless labourers. And the study of Nayar (1975) on the SC and ST high school students also reveals that two-third of fathers of SC and three-fourths of the fathers of ST student worked in the villages. This means that majority of SC and ST students hailed from the poor economic background families. But Nayar's study (1975) further reveals that economically ST students were in more comfortable position than the SC students. With regard to financial assistance provided by the Government, Rajagopalan (1974) found that a majority of ST students complained that they were not getting scholarship due to the unknown reasons and those who were getting the said amount of scholarship was not ade1quate. Nayar (1975) found nearly 80.65 of SC and 79.2 of ST students considered the scholarship as inadequate. However, Sachchidananda (1974 and Singh (1975) found a positive attitude towards governmental help but they also found that most of the SC and ST students expressed dissatisfaction with regard to implementation of these programmes. Thus on the basis of the above findings it can be concluded that poor economic background together with inadequate financial assistance and malfunctioning of the governmental programmes, are the major factors responsible for the slow growth of education among SC and ST students.

In their study on the SC and ST high school students in Guijarat, Desai and Pondor (1974) observed that large number of SC and ST students were first generation learners and majority of SC and ST parents studies upto the primary level of education. Joshi (1981) supported the findings, saying that about 82 per cent of SC and ST fathers had either no education or they had studied upto class IV, and about 95 per cent mothers had practically no education at all. This means that majority of SC and ST parents were illiterate. Naturally this gives rise to a situation where the SC and ST students will not only get improper study atmosphere at home but also the parents show less interest for the education of their children (Joshi-1980). In this study on education among the SC and ST school students in Bihar, Sachchidananda (1974) found that majority of the students had offered arts subjects, because there was lack of facilities for studying science subjects.

Rath (1974) tends to feel that the text books are biased towards culturally advantaged children. The disadvantaged and deprived children who lag behind in language development, generally, do not follow such text books. Such curriculum and text-books tend to accentuate the feelings of alienation in poverty stricken children. Many become alien to school and the school alien to them, coupled with irrelevant curriculum and biased text-book; the non-mother-tongue medium of instruction makes it doubly difficult for deprived children to understand the classroom lessons. For tribal and other categories of economically and culturally backward children, a different medium of instruction can be a strong reason for lack of interest in the school. They are forced to lag behind. This reinforces their alienation and the feeling of incompetence. Further the traditional system of examination in totally outside the realm of experience of the millions of the children from poor homes. The system perpetuates the vested interest in educational stagnation.

Singh (1975), in his study, "Educational Problems of the Scheduled Castes and Scheduled Tribes School Students" mentioned the official measures adopted for their betterment. Vyas and Choudhary (1970) of the Tribal Research Institute and Training Centre, Udaipur (Rajasthan) studied the problems of 'Drop-out in a Tribal Situation'. The major objective of the study was to ascertain the extent and magnitude of wastage and stagnation in education among the students. Joshi (1971) in his doctoral study titled 'The changing pattern of Bhil Life in Banswara', studied the problem of integration of the tribals into the main stream of national life. The results of the study besides discarding the isolationist view, laid emphasis on moulding the official policies with a view to treating the tribals as integral parts of backward communities of the region. Verma (1978) in his book "The Bhil Kills" studied the origin of Bhils, their life and living. Bhuriya (1979) in his compilation "Folk Songs of the Bhils" has collected folk songs representing the values of the Bhil tribe. The investigator has also made a number of studies of the educational problems of tribal students. Mention may be made of "Specific problems of the tribal students studying in the secondary schools of Madhya Pradesh (1977)." "Improving the quality of tribal education (1980)", "A study of Educational Backwardness of Tribal

Students" (1983), "Tribal Children—How to teach them" (1983), "Teaching the Tribal Children" (1983), "A Study of Language Development of Scholastic Achievement and Tribal Students, "Bhil Culture" (Radio Broadcast from Vividh Bharati, 1984), "Chitrashala Programme', 'Reasons of Drop-out of Tribal Children' (1984), and A Study of Educational Backwardness of Tribal Students (1983).

Singh (1975) reported that tribal students lacked awareness of future prospects and had lower preference for technical and professional education. Ameerjan (1984, 1987) also found that the tribal students of B.Sc. (Agriculture) showed significantly lower academic achievement than the non-tribals and their educational aspiration was lower than other students. He further found that the caste subculture and socio-economic level affect the general mental ability and verbal ability.

Mehta (1976) finds that the deprived children lag behind in language development in learning of various concepts and symbols. Recent researcher (Bloom et al, 1965) show that in children growing up under adverse conditions, the IQ may be depressed by 10 to 15 points. For Rath (1976) the subtle psychological and cultural problems of the tribals will stand in the way of their integration. By the time the tribal child comes to primary school at the age of 5 to 6 his cognitive growth is already depressed (Rath, 1974b). The uneducated parent cannot possibly satisfy his natural curiosities about environment. Whatever language is used at home is quite different from the standard language used in the primary schools. The text books used in the schools are written by people belonging to culturally advantaged class, so the concepts and images symbolized in the standard use of words are quite foreign to the tribal children. So when a tribal child comes to class–I and reads the first reader written in the standard language he starts with zero linguistic information and conceptualization, whereas a child belonging to advantaged class has quite a few familiar concepts and linguistic associations in common. This deficiency acquired in class I will accumulate progressively as the child goes through other classes and his accumulated deficiency is ultimately responsible for stagnation, drop-out and weaker motivation for higher education.

Rath (1976) expresses his feelings by stating that in the atmosphere of sub-culture the tribal children may develop low self-esteem and inferiority in comparison with others. This itself may be the single major cause of early drop-out. He (1973) also ascribed weak motivational factors for learning in case of these children which lead to drop-out.

Sharma (1977) has examined the activities of tribal education, the role of teachers in shaping the attitudes of students, types of school building and other allied factors. Mishra (1977) in another book "Role of Education in Tribal Development", published by the Ministry of Home Affairs, Government of India, discusses the nature of tribal education, its changing focus and education for tribals development. Sharma (1978) considers education as one of the most important elements in harnessing the process of change to the advantage of the local community.

In order to understand the personality pattern in relation to culture with particular reference to two Indian hill tribes, viz. the Khasi and the Naga, Sharma (1977) conducted a study. His study revealed culture as a very important factor in moulding one's personality. The two tribes differed significantly in terms of achievement, dominance, conflict, defection, attitude towards religion, intelligence and extraversion – introversion. No significant difference was found in the case of aggression, anxiety and attitude towards life and humanity.

Singh (1979) has related the process of education to social change. The major objective has been access the status of scheduled castes and scheduled tribes and to examine the extent to which education related to social legislation, as well as other forces of modernization, has been effective in eradicating sources of inequality and generating equalization and non-discriminating pattern of relationship. ('Education and Social Change', 1979).

Toppo's (1979) work on "Dynamics of Educational Development in Tribal India", has dealt with the attitude of Oraon students, teachers, parents and guardians towards the formal system of education. Apart from giving several other factors related to the education of Oraon students, he also gives an account of Dhumkuria and the dormitory life of the Oraon young boys.

The study of Arun (1981) showed that the academic achievement of scheduled caste and scheduled tribe students was significantly lower than that of the general population. He further reported that the academic achievement of scheduled tribe students was superior to that of scheduled caste students. Significant correlation between the socio-economic status and the academic achievement scheduled caste and scheduled tribe students was also found.

Kamat (1981) too found that the average scholastic achievement of non-backward class students was significantly better than that of the backward students. Rangari reported that on educational achievement, the non-scheduled caste students did better than the scheduled caste students.

Singh (1981) made an attempt to analyze the academic achievement of the tribal students in relation to their intelligence, level of motivation and personality pattern. It was found that among the tribal students, the lower achievers were more warmhearted, easy going and participating than high achievers. The high achievers tended to be more sober, prudent and serious as well as more practical, careful, conventional and regulated by external realities while the low achievers were more calculating, polished, wordily and shrewd. The tribal pupils, in comparison to the general population, tended to be sober, prudent, serious and dependable. The high achievers tended to be more sober, prudent and serious as well as more practical, careful, conventional and regulated by external realities. The high achieving tribal students in comparison to the general population tended to be less intelligent and emotionally less stable but more jealous, suspicious, withdrawn brooding and hard.

Srivastav (1981) studies the personality patterns of 200 tribals (100 Tharus and 100 Gonds) and 200 non-tribal boys matched on age, education, SES and ecological region, using the Indian adaptation of Cattle's 17 PF Questionnaire, From E. The results showed that the tribal and non-tribal boys differed significantly on factors A (Sociability), C (Egostrength), E (Dominance Vs Submission), G (Super-ego-strength) H (Adventurousness), I (Tough minded Vs. Tender minded), L (Trusting Vs. Suspicious), M (Autia), O-(Guilt Proneness), O-1 (Radicalism) and O-2 (Self sufficiency), O-3 (Self sentiment) and O-(Tension). There was no difference in remaining factors.

Dimaggio (1982) undertook a study to assess the relationship between students interest in and familiarity with high culture and their high school grades. He found that students who participate informal culture and more likely to obtain higher grades in school. This finding was conformed in a follow up study conducted by Dimaggio and Mohr (1985). Their study demonstrated that among secondary school students in the United Sates, participation in high culture has a significant impact on selected attainment measures.

A cross cultural study on personality patterns of tribal and non-tribal students has been undertaken by Panda and Panigrahi (1984) in which they reported that, except in factors C, J and 0-3, tribal and non-tribal students differ significantly in all the remaining eleven factors. Tribal students were found to be less outgoing, less intelligent, emotionally more stable, less active, dominant, happy-go-lucky, shy, little bit tough-minded, depressive (guilt prone), group dependent, had stronger super-ego-strength and high self concept control. Personality factors like outgoing more intelligent, emotionally less stable, overactive, submissive, sober (but serious), socially bold, tender-minded, confident, self sufficient, low self-consent control etc. were found to be the characteristics of non-tribal students. Both the groups were individualistic and frustrated.

In their study on "Social context of Tribal Education" Shah and Patel (1985) observed that, educational development has a positive relationship to the social status of the caste/ communities. The educational development of the tribals was the lowest and that of high caste Hindus was the highest. The educational development of the SC was above ST's but much below that of even the low-caste Hindus. From the community context of educational development of tribals they found a negative relationship between the community contexts (the proportion of the non-tribal population) and the educational development of tribals in a village community, there was a considerable amount of variation in educational attainment as well as social class composition of the different tribal groups. Further, they have concluded that tribals were unaware of the available facilities and special programmes of assistance, hence there was unequal level of development.

Verma (1985) conducted the study with a view to find out whether students from the scheduled tribes differed from the students belonging to scheduled castes with respect to academic achievement, attitude towards school, attitude towards medium of instruction, socio-economic status, self concept and adjustment in school. For the purpose a sample of 1049 students was randomly selected from junior high schools of U.P. of which 557 belonged to STs, 63 belonged to SCs and 429 were from other castes. Some of the major findings were (1) The mean achievement of the scheduled caste students was significantly lower than that of tribal students and students from the other castes. However there was no significant difference in the mean achievement of students belonging to the scheduled tribes and those belonging to other castes. (2) Students from higher castes had a more favourable attitude towards the school when compared to students from the STs and SCs (3) Students from higher castes had a more favourable attitude towards the medium of instruction when compared to students from the STs and SCs (4) The ST students had a higher socio-economic status when compared to students from the SCs and other castes (5) There was no significant difference between tribal and other caste students as regards self-concept. (6) The mean school adjustment score of the tribal group was significantly poorer than that of the non-tribal group. However, there was no significant difference between the mean adjustment score of the SC students and other groups.

Similarly Panda (1986) studied personality adjustment, mental health and acculturation among Saora tribals and found that Oriya and Oriya girls groups possessed better personal adjustment than least-accultured girls. More accultured boys possessed better personal adjustment than least-accultured boys and least-accultured group possessed more psychoticism than more-accultured, and oriya groups. So far as neuroticism was concerned least-accultured groups scored significantly higher than Oriya groups. More extravension was possessed by Oriya group than least-acculturated and more-accultured groups. Further least-accultured students expressed more inferiority feelings than more-accultured (excepting girls) and Oriya (excepting girls) students. Regarding insecurity, Oriya boys possessed more of this trait than more acculturated boys group and least-accultured and least-accultured boys groups. Least accultured and least-acculturated boys groups possessed more fixation in frustration than more acculturated boys and Oriya boys groups. More acculturated boys possessed more aggression than least acculturated boys and Oriya boys. More acculturated boys and least acculturated boys possessed more state-trait anxiety than Oriya boys. Oriya groups displayed increased attitude towards culture change than least acculturated and more acculturated (excepting girls) groups.

Srivastav (1986) conducted a comparative study of tribal and non-tribal stagnates with reference to their mode of stagnation, academic achievement and personality and found that Bhotia and Jaunsari students exhibited a positive attitude towards most of the personality factors. Tharu, Boxa and Raji tribals showed a negative attitude towards personality traits. The stagnates from the Raji tribe had comparatively poor socio-economic background. Bhotia and Jaunsari students showed better academic performance than the non-tribals. Academic performance of Tharu and Raji tribals was inferior to that of the non-tribals.

Sujatha and Yashodhara (1986) in comparative study of some educational variables of SC/ST students found that the SC/ST students were low in their academic achievement and achievement motivation. They had relatively poor school adjustment compared to non-SC/ST students. Both SC/ST and non SC/ST students were low on the personality factor B (less intelligent/more intelligent). And aware average on the other factors, viz C (Affected by feelings/emotionally stable), G (expedient/conscientious) and O2 (Group dependent/self sufficient) of Cattle's HSPO. In case of both SC/ST and non SC/ST groups, academic achievement was found to be independent of achievement motivation and personality factor B,C,G,O2 of HSPO. A significant association between academic achievement and school adjustment was found in the case of SC/ST students, but not in the case of non SC/ST students. In the case of SC/ST as well as non SC/ST groups a significant relationship was found between academic achievement and SES of the students whereas achievement motivation and SES, school adjustment and SES were found to be independent of each other. The personality factor B, G, and O2 in the case of SC/ST and C, G and O2 in the case of non SC/ST were not related to SES but there was a significant relationship between factor C and SES in the case of SC/ST, factor B and SES in case of non SC/ST students. There was a significant association between academic achievement and type of school in the case of SC/ST students. In the case of both SC/ST and non SC/ST students, a significant relationship was found between achievement motivation and type of school, where as school adjustment was found to be independent of the type of school attended. Personality factors, C, G, and O2 in the case of SC/ST students and only G and O2 in the case of non SC/ST students were not dependent on the type of school. Personality factors B and school type were related in the case of both the groups whereas personality factor C and type of schools were related only in the case of non SC/ST students.

In a comparative study on personality and academic achievement of SC and ST college students of Agricultural Sciences, Ameerjan (1987) reported that caste sub-culture and socio-economic level independently affect the level of general mental ability and verbal ability. In the case of non-intellectual variables, the caste sub-culture appears to play a significant role in producing the differences among the groups in respect of economic and religious values, verbalized need for achievement, self-confidence and adjustment to home, educational and social aspects. In the case of extroversion and neuroticism dimensions, neither caste nor socio-economic level has produced significant differences among the groups. The SC and ST students, who as a group are socio-economically disadvantaged when compared to other caste groups have lower general mental ability and verbal ability than the students of other caste groups. Similarly their motivational aspects and adjustment are inadequate. The net effect of these inadequacies was seen on their level of academic achievement which was found to be lower than that of the students of other caste groups.

Patel (1987) studied academic achievement in relation to cognitive and personality differentials of socially disadvantaged and advantaged secondary school children of Orissa and found that all the three groups (viz. SC, ST and the advantaged children) differed significantly in their achievement in academic subjects, intelligence, self-concept, creativity, teacher estimation, linguistic competence and achievement motivation.

Sujatha (1987) undertook a study to find out the underlying causes of absenteeism, stagnation and wastage among Yenadi Tribe. She also studied the effect of socio-economic condition of parents on enrolment of the children and sex difference was also studied. She found that absenteeism was more among Yenadi girls both in mixed villages and tribal colonies; absenteeism was more among Yenadi girls (58.5 %) than the boys (40. 5%) in mixed villages, whereas the difference between girls (27.5%) and boys (25.5%) in tribal colonies was negligible, and absenteeism among

Yenadi boys and girls put together was lower in tribal colonies (26%) than in mixed villages (49.5%).

Recently several studies conducted on scheduled caste and scheduled tribe school students have been reported. They have a common framework. Each of these cover a single state and studies a sample of scheduled caste and scheduled tribe students selected with the help of multi-stage stratified random sampling procedure. They study the students' family and socio-economic background, educational and occupational aspirations, students' life, study habits and performance, problems of interaction with students and teachers, their friends' circle and experience of discrimination (if any), their outlook about the status of scheduled castes and scheduled tribes and attitude towards governmental concession and their administration.

These studies find that most of the scheduled caste and scheduled tribe students are first-generation learners largely coming from poor and illiterate homes where they have to participate a great deal in domestic work and home environment is not congenial for their study. As a result they are slightly older from the class they study in and choose subjects that qualify them for college, where they choose art courses by the large. Though most of them feel that they do well in their studies, a majority of them feel the need for free extra coaching and guidance. Their participation in extra curricular activities remains low, though their educational and occupational aspirations are high. They have become aware politically. A large majority of them remain ethrocantic in their friendship pattern. Most of them think that though the status of the scheduled caste and scheduled tribe groups has improved, it is still inferior to that of the non-scheduled caste groups. Their teachers are of the opinion that they are not inherently low in academic performance as compared to the other students but their unfavourable family environment has made them so. Some of the recent studies are given below.

Mishra (1989) made an attempt to find out the personality patterns and its relationship with academic achievement, educational aspiration and occupational aspiration of SC, ST students studying in Ashram Schools in Orissa and found that school had no significant independent effect on any on the fourteen factors of personality. The academic achievement of the students of non-Ashram school (NAS) was found to be better than that of Ashram Schools. Differences were found only on personality factors E (Obedient VS. Assertive) and F (Sober Vs Enthusiastic) and academic achievement among the different caste groups. Differences between SC and ST group were found only on personality factor E (Obedient Vs. Assertive) and academic achievement. Differences between SC and non-SC/ST groups were found only on personality factors F (Sober Vs. Enthusiastic) and academic achievement. Differences between ST and non-SC/ST were found only on personality factor E (Obedient Vs. Assertive) and academic achievement. Scheduled Tribe students were found to be more assertive, self-assured, independent minded, stern, hostile, solemn, unconventional, rebellious, head-string and admiration demanding as compared to SC and non-SC/ST students. Scheduled caste students were found to be more talkative, cheerful happy-go-lucky, frank, expressive reflecting the group, quick and alert than the non-SC/ST students. In academic achievement the non-SC/ST students were found to be high achievers followed by ST and SC students. Interaction affects were found only on personality factors F, H, O2 and academic achievement.

The relationship of personality factors B (Low intelligence Vs. High intelligence) and C (Affected by feeling Vs. Emotionally stable) was found to be positively related with academic achievement in case of Ashram School ST students. The Ashram School ST and non-Ashram School SC students also exhibited positive relationship of personality factor 03 (uncontrolled Vs. controlled) with academic achievement. Negative relationship of personality factors D (Undemonstrative Vs. Excitable) with academic achievement was revealed in case of Ashram School ST and non-Ashram School ST students. Personality factor O4 (Relaxed Vs. Tense) was found to be negatively related with academic achievement in case of Ashram School ST students.

Sharma (1991) studied educational life style of tribal students and found that the attendance of the pupils was found to be significant with regard to sex and caste, caste and family education, and caste and income. Significant difference with respect to their attendance has been found between tribal and non-tribal pupils. Non-tribal students were more regular in attending the school than the tribals. Further family size and parental occupation of the pupils did not influence the attendance of the pupils. The tribal students had a more positive attitude towards education than the non-tribal students of the sampled group. The tribal students had lower level of educational aspiration than the non-tribal pupils. However the tribal pupils had higher occupational aspiration than the non-tribal pupils. The tribal pupils had obtained more average self-concept score than the non-tribal students. The tribal pupils had lower academic achievement than that of the non-tribal pupils. Further the income of the various caste groups did not influence the academic achievements of the students whether they belonged to higher or lower income groups. Family size did not influence the academic achievement of the students.

Mehta, Bhatnagar and Jain (1993) studied the psycho educational problems of tribal students of Meghalaya and for studying ethnic differences both at the macro and micro levels, they included a group of non-tribal high schools students and three tribes namely Khasi, Mizo and Garo living in around Shillong respectively. Ethnic differences at the macro level showed that the tribal and non-tribals differed at 5% level of significance on aggregate marks, the non-tribals having higher mean score than the tribals. Among boys however, ethnic differences were not evident on the aggregate marks. The tribal and non-tribal girls differed at 1% level of significance the non-tribal girls having higher mean achievement than the tribal girls. Further it was observed that the non-tribals generally also got higher marks than the tribals in individual subjects. Increase or fall of score for tribals and non-tribals respectively suggested that the tribals belonging to the lower SES showed poor academic achievement whereas the non-tribals of higher SES revealed high academic achievement. It was further achieved that in spite of similar facilities at home for studies, tribals were lower on academic achievement than the non-tribals. The tribals and non-tribals differ at 5% level in achievement in science subjects, with the non-tribals getting higher marks, than the tribals. Ethnic micro-level comparison showed that the three tribes belonging to the five comparison groups did not differ on most of the school subjects and aggregate of marks after partialling out age and SES simultaneously. The three tribes belonging to rural group differed at 1% level on the achievement in Mathematics after partialling out age and SES simultaneously. The inspection of means of the group indicated that Garos found mathematics difficult in comparison to Khasis and Mizos. Tribal/FGL (First Generation Learner) and NFGL (Non-first generation learner) pooled groups did not differ significantly on any of the achievement scores except on mathematics, on which the groups differed at 5% levels of significance, with the FGL having higher mean score than the NFGL. The FGL had marginally higher score in all subjects than the NFGL except in Hygiene and in Garo and Mizo languages. Age and SES of FGL and NFGL had a marginal effect on their school achievement. Sex differences among the tribal FGL showed up at 5% levels of significance on achievement in only two subjects viz. science and hygiene. In general FGL boys had marginally higher achievement scores than the girls. Age and SES of FGL boys and girls had no significant bearing on their school achievement.

Mishra (1996) conducted a study on "Education of Tribal Children". The findings are as follows:

1. So far as the area (Hilly Vs. Plain) and the level of drop-out (high Vs. low) schools were concerned there was no association between the phenomenon of drop-out and all the ten psychological variables.

2. In comparison between high and low drop-out schools in the highly area, there was association between drop-out and intelligence, academic motivation, level of aspiration, inferiority, insecurity, and school adjustment. The low drop-out students did possess lower inferiority and insecurity and higher on the rest of the four variables than the high drop-out students in the hilly area.

3. Within a plain area, drop-out was found associated with only school adjustment, and the low drop-out students did have higher adjustment than the high drop-out students in the plain area.

4. Between high drop-outs of hilly and plain area, drop-out was associated with academic motivation and lower inferiority than high drop-out hilly area students.

5. No association between drop-out and the psychological variables was found in case of low drop-out students from hilly area (LDH) Vs. low drop-out students from plain area (LDP) and low dıop-out students from hilly area (LDHP). Vs. plain area students.

6. Illiteracy of parents was a reasonable factor related to the school drop-out phenomenon.

7. Lack of parental awareness towards education of child led him/her to become a drop-out.

8. The incidence of highest drop-out was in case of nuclear family.

9. Lack of control of parents over the children led them to become drop-out.

10. Harsh behaviour of the parents was a major factor behind the drop-outs in hilly area.

11. Education did not help the students in future; so dropped out.

12. Lack of family support in Government Schools (HA) was a factor behind the drop-out phenomenon.

13. Engagement of children in some work, inside or outside home led to school drop-out.
14. Economic backwardness of the family did not permit the children to continue their studies and thus drop-out.
15. Engagement of drop-outs in paid work to supplement the family income was a cause of school drop-out.
16. Failure of education to increase the prestige of the parents was still another factor of drop-out.
17. Lack of encouragement by the community led to drop-out.
18. Payment of dowry was responsible for girls' drop-outs.
19. Parental hesitation to send the girls to co-educational institutions was a factor in girls' drop-outs.
20. Improper school timings/schedule led the students to drop-out from the school.
21. Irregularity of teachers in attending to the school was a factor behind the sense of school drop-out.
22. Lack of interest of teachers led students to drop-out from the school.
23. Lack of adequate physical facilities in the school was a major factor responsible for drop-out phenomenon.
24. Unsuitable and heavy curriculum led the students to drop-out from the school.
25. Lack of healthy school-community relationship was responsible for the phenomenon of school drop-out.
26. Due to medium of instruction other than the tribals own, caused students to drop-out from the school.
27. Students drop-out from the school due to high teacher pupil ratio.
28. Another major source of school drop-outs was lacks of trained and qualified teachers.

29. Students drop-out could be ascribed to lack of large number of teachers being drawn from the tribal community.

The study of Mishra (1998) reveals the following findings:

(i) The high achievers of Ashram Schools were found to be reserved, emotionally less stable, less active, submissive, persistent, tough-minded, zestful and have high self-concept control in comparison to the high achievers of non-Ashram Schools.

(ii) The low achievers of Ashram Schools, when compared to low achievers of non-Ashram Schools were found to be reserved, emotionally less stable, submissive, sober, tough-minded, apprehensive and have high self concept control.

(iii) The high achievers of Ashram Schools in comparison to low achievers of non-Ashram School possessed the personality traits like less outgoing, more intelligence, emotionally less stable, inactive, sober, persistent, tough-minded, zestful, apprehensive and have high self-concept control.

(iv) The SC high achievers in comparison to the non-SC/ST achievers seem to be more enthusiastic, shy, tender-minded and sociable-group dependent than their ST high achievers counterparts.

(v) The non-SC/ST high achievers when compared to the SC high achievers were found to be more intelligent, have stronger super ego strength, adventurous, tough-minded and self-sufficient. The ST high achievers in comparison to the non-SC/ST high achievers counterpart were found to be less intelligent and have weaker super ego strength.

(vi) The SC low achievers in comparison to the ST low achievers were less intelligent, enthusiastic, have weaker super ego strength and reflective. But the SC low achievers when compared to the non-SC/ST low achievers were found to be less outgoing, less intelligent, emotionally less stable, inactive, tough-minded and tense.

(vii) The ST low achievers were reserved, less intelligent, emotionally less stable, tough minded, zestful, apprehensive and tense when compared to their non-SC/ST low achievers counterparts.

(viii) The SC high achievers in comparison to the ST low achievers were found to be out going, happy-go-lucky have weaker super ego strength, shy and sociably group dependent. On the other hand, the comparison of SC high achievers with that of non-SC/ST high achievers indicates that the SC high achievers were happy-go-lucky, shy, tough minded, zestful, apprehensive, sociably group dependent, have high self-concept control and tense.

(ix) When the ST high achievers were compared with the non-SC/ST low achievers, it was found that the ST high achievers were comparatively less outgoing, emotionally less stable, inactive, tough minded, zestful, apprehensive and have high self-concept control.

(x) The school has no significant independent effect on the personality factors like G (Expedient Vs. Conscientious), Q2 (Sociably Group dependent Vs. Self sufficient) and Q4 (Relax Vs. Tense). Difference between the student of Ashram schools and non-Ashram schools were found on eleven personality factors (i.e. A, B, C, D, E, F, G, H, I, J, O and Q3). The students of Ashram School were more intelligent adventurous,

apprehensive and controlled whereas the students of non-Ashram schools were more easy going, emotionally stable, excitable, competitive, enthusiastic, tender-minded and internally restrained.

(xi) The main effect of caste was significant on eleven personality factors like. A, B, C, D, E, F, G, J, O, Q2, Q3 and Q4. The significant mean difference indicated that the ST students were more intelligent, conscientious, self-sufficient, controlled and frustrated than the SC students. The SC students were more enthusiastic and reflective than the ST students. When SC students were compared with their non-SC/ST counterparts it was found that the non-SC/ST students were more outgoing, more-intelligent, emotionally stable, impatient, persistent and controlled, whereas the SC students were more enthusiastic, apprehensive and frustrated. When the ST students were compared with their non-SC/ST counterparts, it was found that the non-SC/ST students were more easy going, more intelligent, emotionally stable, impatient and reflective while the ST students were comparatively more apprehensive, controlled and frustrated.

(xii) Interaction effects of school and caste were found on personality factor like A, B, C, D, E, F, H, I, O, Q3 and Q4. The ASSC group had a higher mean score in the personality factor A (i.e. Reserved Vs, Warm Hearted) than their ASST group counterparts, but had a lower mean score than their NASSC, NASST and NASN SC/ST group counterparts. The ASN SC/ST and ASST groups had a lower mean score on this personality factor as compared to NASSC, NASST and NASN SC/ST groups.

Further, the NASSC group had a lower mean score as compared to NASN SC/ST and NASST while the NASSC/ST had a higher mean score on this factor—A as compared to NASST group.

(xiii) The ASSC and NASSC students differed significantly on personality factors like A (i.e. reserved Vs. outgoing), B (i.e. less intelligent Vs. more intelligent), D (i.e. Inactive Vs. impatient) and F (i.e. Sober Vs. Enthusiastic). The ASSC students were found to be reserved, more intelligent, inactive and sober.

(xiv) The ASST and NASST students differed on personality factors A, B, C, D, E, F, I, O, and Q4. The ASST students were found to be reserved, more intelligent, emotionally less stable inactive, obedient, sober, tough minded, apprehensive and relaxed.

(xv) Differences between AS non-SC/ST and NAS non-SC/ST groups were found on personality factors A (Reserved Vs. Warm hearted), B (Less intelligent Vs. More intelligent), C (Affected by feelings Vs. Emotionally stable), I (Obedient Vs. Assertive), H (Shy Vs. Adventurous), T (Though-minded Vs. Tender minded), O (Self-Assured Vs. Apprehensive) and Q3 (Uncontrolled Vs. Controlled). The AS non-SC/ST students were revealed to be reserved, less intelligent, emotionally less stable, obedient, adventurous, tough-minded, apprehensive and have high self-concept control.

(xvi) The ASSC and NASST students differed on seven personality factors like A, B, C, D, E, O and Q4. The ASSC students tend to be reserved more intelligent, emotionally less stable, inactive, obedient, apprehensive and relaxed. Differences between ASSC and NASNSC/ST groups were revealed on personality factors

A, B, C, D, E, H, I, O, Q3 and Q4. The NASNSC/ST students were warm-hearted, more intelligent, emotionally stable, overactive dominant, shy, tender-minded, self-assured, uncontrolled and relaxed.

(xvii) The ASSC and ASST students differed only on personality factors A, B, F, and O. The ASST students were found to be reserved, more intelligent, sober and apprehensive.

(xviii) The ASSC and ASN SC/ST student differed on personality factors D, E, H, I and Q4. The ASN SC/ST students were revealed to be impatient, submissive, adventurous, tough-minded and relaxed.

(xix) Difference on personality factors A, B, C, D, F, I, O and Q3 were revealed between ASST and NASSC students. The NASSC students were found to be easy going, less intelligent, emotionally stable, impatient, enthusiastic, sensitive, complacent and have low integration than the ASST students.

(xx) The ASST and NASNCS/ST students differed on personality factors A, B, C, D, E, F, H, I, O, Q3 and Q4. The ASST, students were found to be reserved, less intelligent, emotional, less stable, inactive, submissive, sober, adventurous, tough-minded, apprehensive, controlled and frustrated than NASNSC/ST students.

(xxi) Difference between ASST and ASNSC/ST groups were noted on personality factors B, D, E, F, H and O. The ASNSC/ST students were revealed to be less intelligent, impatient, submissive, enthusiastic, adventurous and self assured than ASST students.

(xxii) ASNSC/ST and NASSC students differed on personality factors A, B, F, H, I and Q3. The

NASSC students were found to be out-going, less intelligent, enthusiastic, shy, tender-minded and have low integration than ASNSC/ST students.

(xxiii) Difference between ASNSC/ST and NASST groups were observed on personality factors A, B, C, D, E, F, I, O, and Q4. The NASST students were revealed to be outgoing, less intelligent, emotionally stable, impatient, dominant, happy-go-lucky, tender-minded, self assured and tense.

(xxiv) The NASSC and NASN SC/ST students differed on personality factors A, B, C, D, E, F, I and O. The NASSC students in comparison to NASNSC/ST students were found to be reserved, less intelligent, emotionally less stable, inactive, obedient, happy-go-lucky, tough-minded and apprehensive.

(xxv) Differences on personality factors A, B, C, D, E, F, H, O, Q3 and Q4 were noted between NASSC and NASST students. The NASST students were found to be outgoing, more intelligent, emotionally stable, overactive, dominant, sober, adventurous, complacent, have high self-concept control and frustrated than NASSC students.

(xxvi) The NASST and NASNSC/ST students differed on personality factors A, B, C, E, F, H, I, Q3 and Q4. In comparison to NASST students, the NASNSC/ST students were found to be outgoing, more intelligent, emotionally stable, competitive, sober, shy, tender-minded, have low integration and relaxed.

(xxvii) There was no independent effect of school on the academic achievement of students.

(xxviii) Caste had significant effect on the academic achievement of students. Difference between SC and ST and SC and non-SC/ST groups were found to be significant on academic achievement. In academic achievement the non-SC/ST students were found to be high achievers followed by ST and SC students.

(xxix) The school and caste had joint effects on the academic achievement of students. Differences between ASSC and NASSC, ASSC and NASN SC/ST, ASSC and ASST, ASST and NASSC, ASST and ASNSC/ST, ASNSC/ST and NASSC ASNSC/ST and NASN SC/ST and NASSC and NASNSC/ST groups were found to be significant on academic achievement. In academic achievement the ASSC students excelled the NASSC students. On the other hand, the ASST students excelled the ASSC, NASSC and ASNSC/ST students in achievement. The ASN SC/ST students were found to be higher in academic achievement than the NASSC students. The NASST students were appeared to be higher than NASSC, ASNSC/ST and ASSC students and lower than the ASST and NASN SC/ST students in academic achievement.

(xxx) Majority of SC and ST students were from low socio-economic background.

(xxxi) The SC, ST students were poor in academic subjects like mathematics G.Sc. and English.

THE PRESENT STUDY IN RELATION TO THE ABOVE LITERATURE

The literature pertaining to the present study has been studied at length by the investigator. The foreign studies were conducted on culturally disadvantaged, backwards, socially disadvantaged and psycho- socially disadvantaged. The Indian studies depicted the precarious multidimensional educational problems. The problems arise out of the poor socio-economic conditions, culture, poverty, educational system and administrative pattern. The studies on the variables of achievement coincide with the evidences of foreign studies, pointing to the triabls and harijans about the low scholastic achievement, low level of intelligence, weak aspiration level and adverse personality pattern. Studies are very few which speak about their superiority. The other Indian studies stated their education in schools despite their deplorable socio-economic and educational status. The SC and ST students are backward in the eyes of their teachers. Three studies speak about the benefits of Ashram schools and some studies recommended the open organizational climatic school for tribals.

The above studies were done mostly on primary school children. The studies do not give any compact picture of student achievement of tribal and harijans. Since independence several special schools have been opened in different states. There are no systematic study on these schools to verify their achievement in educating the tribal and harijan children. The investigator has come across a very few studies on tribal schools about n-achievement and personality pattern. Those studies do not tell about the basic variables of students' educational progress. However, those studies help the investigator in getting a psychosocial picture. It is, therefore, in fitness of things that the present study aims at filling a research gap by way of studying factors associated with students achievement of Ashram schools.

3

DESIGN OF THE STUDY

The previous chapter deals with the review of related literature pertaining to the present investigation. Precise formulation of the research problem, relevant hypotheses and appropriate assumptions have been incorporated in the first chapter. The present chapter embodies the design of the study, which includes a brief description of the method, population and sample, tools, data collection procedure, and the statistical techniques employed for conducting the present study.

METHOD

Hillway (1956) mentions "If the scholar can not clearly describe his method, the chances are that it is too vague and general to yield him satisfactory results". So there is need to describe the method used in research work. The decision about the methods depends upon the nature of the problems selected, the kind of data necessary and its objectives. Keeping in view the above rationale the investigator chooses the method for her study. The present study has been planned and implemented under a descriptive and cross sectional framework. Best (1978) states: Descriptive research describes and interprets what is. It is concerned with conditions or relationships that exist; practices that prevail; beliefs, points of view or attitudes that are held; process that are being felt; or trends that are developing.

Of course descriptive research goes beyond mere collection of data and tabulating them. It involves meaningful analysis of the data and drawing out the relevant inferences and significant conclusions. Hence, description of the investigation is obviously combined with analysis, comparison, contrast, interpretation and evaluation. Descriptive studies collect and provide three types of information: *(i)* of what exists with respect to variables or conditions in a situation, *(ii)* of what we want by identifying standards or norms with which to compare the present conditions or what experts consider to be desirable, and *(iii)* of how to achieve goals by exploring possible ways and means on the basis of the experience of others or the opinions of experts.

So far as the research methodology is concerned, the present study comes under the scope of "Descriptive Research". This is a status study of descriptive nature made on the basis of data gathered through field investigation. So the method, to be more exact, followed in this study was said to be the "Descriptive Survey' under "Causal Comparative" one.

This study would explore the causal relationship among samples those are different on the critical variable like School type (i.e. independent variable), but otherwise comparable on the basis of student achievement (i.e. dependent variable).

POPULATION AND SAMPLE

In research, population refers to any defined whole or aggregate. It is the basis for arriving at the parameter of the study. As such the importance of defining population of a study may be readily seen.

The present study has been conducted on Harijan and Tribal Welfare Department High Schools and Education Department High Schools in Orissa. The study started in August, 1997. So the population consists of such High schools in full operation in 1997-98. For the purpose of effective administration, the state of Orissa is divided into three revenue divisions, namely Northern, Central, and Southern. The present study was designed to compare two types of schools, namely Harijan and Tribal Welfare Schools and Education Department High Schools distributed over three revenue divisions in 13 undivided districts of Orissa.

Relevant information have to be collected from the students studying in grade X. Thus, to be more exact, population in the present study constituted the X graders studying in both HTW and Education Department high schools. The reasons for selecting the grade X students are: firstly to avoid the effects of prematurity in the childhood stage; and secondly such students were to appear in the Annual High School Certificate Examination 1999 conducted by the Board of Secondary Education, Orissa which would be uniform for all and would facilitate in obtaining their marks indicative of academic achievement.

In order to get a representative sample, it was thought of to have at least two districts to be drawn from each revenue division. Thus six districts viz. Ganjam and Phulbani from Southern zone, Cuttack and Dhenkanal from Central zone and Balasore and Keonjhar from Northern zone were selected randomly for the present investigation. Further 13 Ashram High Schools were randomly selected from the six districts out of total listed Ashram High Schools of those districts having grade X during the session 1997-98. All the students reading in grade X of the selected schools formed one part of the sample. All the selected 13 schools were Government High Schools under the control of Harijan and Tribal Welfare Department of Orissa.

In order to get a representative sample from the non-Ashram Schools 12 Government High Schools under the control of Education Department of Orissa were randomly selected out of the total listed High Schools situated in the areas from where Ashram Schools were selected. This was done with the purpose of ensuring equality in geographical location of Ashram and non-Ashram schools. This formed the other part of the sample.

The total sample comprised 1000 students out of which 394 ST, 74 SC and 62 non-SC/ST students (i.e. N=530) were from the Ashram schools; and 16 ST, 42 SC and 412 non-ST/SC students (i.e. N=470) were from the Non-Ashram Schools (i.e. Education Department schools). A list of the selected high schools along with the districts to which they belong and the number of students belonging to different groups is given in Table 3.1.

In order to compare the school facilities, relevant data are to be collected from the heads of the sample schools. Thus the sample consisted of 13 Head Masters/Head Mistresses of Ashram schools and 12 Headmasters/Headmistresses of Education Department High Schools.

TOOLS USED

The following data gathering instruments have been used in the present study to collect the data:

1. Socio-Economic Status Scale by Kamila (1985) was used to collect the data on socio-economic status. This scale has been constructed particularly for the people from lowest Social class.

2. Secondary Schools Facilities Survey Questionnaire developed by the investigator was used to measure the school facilities.

3. An Attitude Scale was developed by the investigator and used for the purpose.

4. Occupational Aspiration Scale by Grewal (1984) was used to measure the occupational aspirations of the students.

5. Educational Aspiration Scale developed by Sharma and Gupta (1980), translated into Oriya by Mishra (1990) was used to measure the educational aspirations of the students.

6. Achievement Motivation Inventory standardised by Mehta (1969) was used for the purpose.

7. Achievement Score.

A brief description of these tools have been given in the following pages.

Table 3.1: District-wise, School-wise and Caste-wise Distribution of Sample Students

Name of the District	*Name of the Schools (Ashram)*	*Number of Students*			*Total*
		SC	*ST*	*Non SC/ST*	
Ganjam	Nimakhandi Ashram School	23	21	13	57
	Mohana Ashram School	01	34	—	35
Phulbani	Daringbadi Ashram School	05	18	17	40
	Kotagarh Ashram School	04	46	—	50
	Badgaon Ashram School	04	36	—	40
Keonjhar	Trilochanpur Ashram School	03	34	03	40
	Naranpur Ashram School	03	22	05	30
Dhenkanal	Tarinipasi Ashram School	10	40	01	51
	Damasala Ashram School	01	19	—	20
Balasore	Kabatghati Ashram School	01	42	06	49
	Banabhuin Ashram School	05	37	06	48
Cuttack	Chandikhol Ashram School	09	32	09	50
	Tamaka Ashram School	05	13	02	20
	Total	**74**	**394**	**62**	**530**

Name of the District	*Name of the Schools (Education Department)*	*Number of Students*			*Total*
		SC	*ST*	*Non SC/ST*	
Ganjam	Queen Mission School, Berhampur	01	—	49	50
	Govt. H.S., Mohana	04	—	20	24
Phulbani	Lalbahadur Sastri High School, Daringbadi	02	02	27	31
	Girls High School, Baliguda	02	02	20	24
Keonjhar	Balaram High School, Puruna Bandha Goda	07	03	27	37
	Naranpur High Schools	04	02	24	30
Dhenkanal	Alutuma High School, Kamakhya Nagar	03	03	44	50
	Palasapithia High School	03	—	47	50
Balasore	Jaleswar High School	02	01	48	51
	K.C. High School, Nilagiri	01	—	40	41
Cuttack	Aswatha Pal High School	10	—	22	32
	Kalakala High School	03	03	44	50
	Total	**42**	**16**	**412**	**470**

Kamila's Socio-Economic Status Scale

To measure the socio-economic status of students for verification of hypothesis one (i.e. 1.7.1.) the data on variable of SES of parents were necessary. Many variables have been identified in relation to social status. In India social status is attached to the amount of the income as well as the source of income, occupation, education, prestige, the amount of land in possession, type of houses and the ownership of materials etc.

Several scales have been developed in foreign countries to measure socio-economic status. Some of the important scales are Chapin (1928), Taussing (1928) Cattell (1942), Sims (1952) Warner et al (1949) and Hollinghead and Redlich (1958).

Similarly in India many scholars have attempted to develop the SES scale to measure socio-economic status. To name a few are Kuppuswamy (1959), Rahudkar (1960), Verma (1962), Pareek and Trivedi (1964), Kulshrestha (1973), Srivastava (1975) Rao (1977) and Kamila (1985).

The aforesaid tools except Kamila (1985) are constructed for either rural or urban families. None of the composite scales for both the area are on the selected variable of the present study and these scale except Kamila's (1985) have little scope to measure the SES of the people from lowest social class. Hence the SES scale developed by Kamila (1985), which is comprehensive and appropriate in the present context, has been selected. It consists of seven sub-scales, namely, (I) Sub-scale A: Education, (II) Sub-scale B: Occupation, (III) sub-scale C: Income (IV) sub-scale D: Land, (V) sub-scale E: Social participation, (VI) sub-scale F: House and (VII) sub-scale G: Material possession. The total score of all sub-scales were the indicator of socio-economic status. The total score may vary from 08 to 56. Mean and S.D. of the distribution were calculated to classify the social class on five point scale. The explanation of the social class has been given in Table 3.2.

Table 3.2: Assignment of Social Class

Symbol	*Range of scores on the scale*	*Category*
A	40 or above	Upper class
B	31-39	Upper middle class
C	22-30	Middle class
D	13-21	Lower middle class
E	12 or below	Lower class

EVALUATION OF THE SCALE

(a) Reliability of the Scale

The stability of the scale was determined by the test-retest method. The scale was administered to 100 students of four schools twice at an interval of two months. The stability coefficient of sub-scales except social participation and whole scale were computed separately by Pearson Product Moment Method of Correlation (Table 3.3). Table 3.3 indicates the high reliability coefficient of each sub-scale and scale which is the indicator of high reliability of the scale.

Table 3.3: Test-Retest Reliability Co-efficient of SES Scale

Reliability Coefficient	*Sub-Scales*						
	Edn	*Occupation*	*Income*	*Land*	*House*	*Material possession*	*Scale*
	0.947	0.893	0.681	0.762	0.823	0.716	0.792

(b) Validity of the Scale

The following methods were used to find the validity of the scale:

Content Validity

The content validity of the scale was borne out by the method of collecting items. The universe of the concept was covered widely and sampled through interviews with the various persons—service holders, farmers and other householders, experts, outside persons knowing the population well, and Indian and foreign studies.

Concurrent Validity

The concurrent validity of the scale was tested by comparing the score of the scale correspond to outside criterion. In this case some well-identifiable groups were taken as criterion.

A random sample of homogeneous group of 25 persons from two villages taking at least 10 from a village were asked to name five persons well-known to him and categories them in social class they belong on five point. In this way social class of 89 persons were obtained. Then the scale was administered on those 89 persons. The scales were scored to get their social class.

Taking two sets of obtained social class of 89 persons 'C' in 5 x 5 table was calculated and the value was .816 which indicates the high concurrent validity of the tool.

The scale was scored according to score assigned to each scale point and the scores on each sub-scale are entered in the square by the side of each sub-scale. The social class category was entered on the top square of the scale booklet.

Secondary School Facilities Survey Questionnaire

In order to verify the hypothesis (i.e. 1.7.2), the data on available physical, teaching and economic facilities of secondary schools convertible to scores were necessary. For the purpose, Secondary Schools Facilities Survey Questionnaire was developed by the investigator in the light of Kamila (1985). There are several tools (i.e. Morrison and Ruegsegger, 1943; NESI, 1942 and N.C.E.R.T. 1982) which evaluate school practice, classroom climate and teaching practice. But these tools do not tell a little about the measurement of facilities.

The SSFSQ consists of 13 items. These items relate to type of school building, school campus, furniture, type of rooms available, teaching aids, equipments, audio-visual aids, subjects taught, common facilities, hostel facilities, tutorial arrangement, number of personnel working in the school and landed property of the school.

EVALUATION OF THE TOOL

The reliability and validity of the tool were determined by the following methods:

Test-retest Reliability

The questionnaires were administered on 20 headmasters (i.e. 10 TW and 10 Education department) twice with a gap of two months. The item numbers from 12 to 13 consists of recording number and amount. The headmasters mentioned the same twice in giving the numbers and amount of money in item numbers 12 to 13, which showed high reliability of these items. The reliability co-efficient of eleven items were computed separately by Pearsons' Product Moment Correlation which is given in Table 3.4.

Table 3.4: Reliability Coefficient of Different Items of Secondary School's Facilities Survey Questionnaire

Reliability	1	2	3	4	5	6	7	8	9	10	11
coefficient	.90	.89	.74	.68	.71	.73	.94	.80	.81	.87	.94

VALIDITY OF SSFSQ

Content Validity

The items were collected through a replicated pilot survey of the schools and in consultation with available literature and experts in educational management and organization. This shows the inclusiveness of the universe of the concept. During the tryout the headmasters did not suggest any changes. The above discussions tell about the high content validity of the items as well as the instrument as a whole.

The SSFSQ was scored according to score assigned to each scale point.

Attitude Scale

To verify hypothesis 1.7.3 the data in scores on attitude towards different areas are necessary. However, the concept of "attitude" has been defined operationally in Chapter-I. Attempts have been made to measure attitude of the students (Rao, 1970); Sodhi, 1972; Kamila 1985; and Manava, 1988). But these scales were not suitable for the present sample. Hence the investigator decided to construct a scale.

METHODS OF MEASUREMENT OF ATTITUDES

Measurement of attitudes of a group of people or of an individual is a complex affair. Davis (1972) admitted that "although attempts to measure attitudes have been more successful than have attempts to define them, it does not follow that attitudes are measured easily" and that certain empirical conditions must be satisfied if attitude measurement is to occur. Edwards (1957) has also observed that "when a research worker is interested in measuring the attitudes of a large number of individuals, he may find that there is no available scale suitable for his purpose. It thus becomes necessary for him to his own scale".

There are several methods of attitude measurement. Some of them are the methods of paired comparison, the successive intervals and summated rating; scalogram analysis, direct rating method and method of direct questioning and reports on past and intended behaviour. Some of them are discussed below.

Method of Equal-appearing Intervals

The most widely used technique of measuring the positivity of attitude is Thurstone's method of equal appearing interval.

The outstanding features of this method is that the decisions of a large number of judges are used for determining the points on the attitude continuum.

After collecting a large number of statements which express various degrees of positive and negative attitude towards the object in question, a number of judges are asked to arrange them in a continuum rating from most favourable through 'neutral' to 'most unfavourable'. It is expected that the attitude of respective judges are not to be reflected in their rating but their decisions regarding the intensity of each statement. The index of scale-value of a statement is one-half of the distance between the 25th and 75th percentage of the judges rating. Statements having low inter-judges variability are retained. From those statements a group which spreads evenly over the continuum are selected on the basis of the medium score. The statements are then ordered randomly to make the final scale. The scale is used by asking the judges to select those statements with which he agrees. The attitude score is composed by taking into account the medium score-value of the item with which agrees.

The use of judges for ordering the statements on a continuum has both advantage and disadvantage. The advantage is that we have scale positions, which is of utmost importance in science of measurement. The low inter-judge variability ensures precision of the scale-values. The location of neutral point by the decision of judges is another advantage. But all those advantages will be of practical value if the judgements of intensity are independent of the attitudes of judges. Otherwise different groups of judges will give different scale positions and the neutral point will not remain neutral any more. However the investigations carried out by Hinckley (1932) showed that the relative position of statements on the scale are often unaffected by the use of different groups of judges, but there are slight differences in the rating of the intensity of the statement. In another study, Beyle (1932) also reported the same view.

A most important question is raised about the intervals at the extreme ends. Shaw and Wright (1927) states. "Intervals at the extremes are compressed relative to intervals near the middle of the scale," and according to Hevnes (1930) the intervals of the equal method scale are not equal.

We are not also sure that there are sufficient items to be sorted at the extreme intervals. This also has something to do to affect the scale position. Another condition to be satisfied for the method is that the items should be monotone. But the method of selection of items in to find the value which is not sufficient to purify the scale.

Method of Summated Rating

The method of summated rating is popularly known as the Likert method of scale construction and it follows the simple procedure of psychological test.

For this method we require a large number of monotone statements which can be grouped distinctly as favourable and unfavourable with approximately the same number of the statements in each class. The statements are then taken together to form the scale measuring attitude. During administration, the subjects are asked to respond to the statements on a five point or three point scale. In this method the statements regarding the attitude object providing response and the subjects are automatically divided among themselves in different groups according to their respective degree of favourableness or unfavourableness towards attitude object.

More over in the Likert method, the subjects are allowed more freedom to respond to a five point rating scale and thus they are provided to show intensity of their reaction, whereas in the Thurstone method, they are permitted either to agree or to disagree.

The principle of the interpretation of the score is that the individuals having more favourable attitude towards the object will have more scores. For the final selection of items, each item score is correlated with total score.

Items having high correlation are selected for the attitude scale.

This method of construction of scale has some significance. Green (1954) suggested that inter-correlation of item signify that all the items measure the common factor, the general attitude with a large number of items, the liner correlation approaches unity signifying that the item factors or errors are reduced.

According to Shaw and Wright (1927), "Likert type of scales are often reliable and valid but they probably should be treated as ordinal scale".

Ferguson (1969) stated about the summated ratings that Likert because he found a higher validity co-efficient with his method of scoring rather than with the equal appearing method of scoring erroneously concluded that "his technique is better one". The Likert type of scales with ever fewer statements will give higher reliability co-efficient as indicated by Hall. Reliability co-efficient of his scale of 10 statements measuring attitude towards religion ranged from 0.91 to 0.93.

One thing we are to note that score of an individual has meaning only in relation to scores earned by other member of the sample. Thus within a population range where the test has been standardized, an individual's score can be interpreted as belonging to higher group, or lower group or middle group and be utilized profitably for required purpose. At the same time it is also admitted that in absence of a neutral or a zero point in the continuum of Likert type, it is very difficult to describe a subject as having favourable and unfavourable attitude.

Method of Socio-gram

This procedure has been adopted by Guttman and is a marked departure from the other methods of constructing attitude scales. More correct by speaking the object of this method is not to construct a scale but to test whether a set of statements "can be scaled on an attitude continuum".

What is done is that a set of statements which represent with varying intensity of attitude to an object is collected and arranged in such a fashion as the most favourable statement is '2' and so on. It is assumed that this ordering of statements fall along a single dimension and that an individual agreeing to a more extreme item will also agree with the less extreme items also. One is not sure at the beginning whether a set of statements could be arranged in such a fashion but if the responses of subjects to the statements are accord with our theoretical model of undimensional scale of statements, we could have confidence in interpreting scores of subjects leased upon the statements as also falling along the same undimensional continuum.

The concept of undimensional scalability in turns of same ordering of persons and items as suggested by Guttman is highly appealing, but it is not convenient from the view point of practicability. According to June (1959) "when the criterion not met perfectly, and it is highly unlikely that it ever will be, there is a little that can be done statistically to determine number and kinds of scale which underlie the responses".

After verifying the various techniques and examining the comments on them it was found that Likert technique which is simple yet equally reliable and with which the contribution of various area of attitude can also be compared was the most suitable. In the current investigation the Likert technique was accepted.

PURPOSE OF CONSTRUCTION OF THE TOOL

The following purposes were kept in view to construct the scales:

To construct attitude scale of Likert type taking school, teacher, class-mate and curriculum as attitude objects to compare the attitude of statements of Harijan and Tribal Welfare Department and Education Department High Schools.

ASSUMPTIONS UNDERLYING THE CONSTRUCTION OF TOOL

The measurement of psychological traits or variables means the description of data in terms of numbers. According to Campbell (1940) measurement means the "assignment of scores to objects or events according to rules". In case of measuring attitude, "we assign numerical to persons according to a set of rules that are intended to create an isomorphism between the assigned scores and the persons attitude towards the object in question".

According to our conceptualization of the construct attitude of the individuals do not manifest themselves in overt responses but serve as an intervening variable. So one is to adopt indirect methods for measuring them. This may be done by asking the individuals to respond to a set of situations, keeping in view that the other determinants of behaviour, situational or dispositional, should be neutralized as far as practicable. This can be done by assuring the subjects that their responses will be kept strictly confidential and by adopting such other methods as well be required in specific situation, the set of situations can be provided by a set of statements which include various concepts regarding the attitude-object. The statement should be selected in such a way as those might represent conceptual relations with the object from different perspectives. As the subjects will try to respond to the statement, their conceptual relations with the attitude object will easily be evoked and will react accordingly. Thus their response tendencies will be manifested as they will select the different categories of 'agreement' and 'disagreement'. Then the assessment of the evaluative responses to the statements will be the indication of the attitude of the subjects.

CONSTRUCTION OF THE ATTITUDE SCALE

The following steps were followed to construct the attitude scale:

I. To collect a large number of statements a random sample of 60 class-X students of four randomly selected High Schools were asked to write 10 sentences on school, teacher, classmate and curriculum and separately. The sentences were analyzed and a large number of statements were collected. Also statements were collected from educationists, lecturers, headmasters and M. Ed students and review of literature in mentioned areas.

II. Scrutiny for Relevance and Editing the Statements

The collected statements were scrutinized for irrelevance, duplications and overlapping. Then the scrutinized statements were shown to five lecturers and Readers of RIE, Bhubaneswar and five language experts to check for ambiguity, vagueness, doubtfulness, factuality, irrelevance and unanimous acceptance or rejection and language difficulty. On the basis of their suggestions some statements were rejected and some modified. One hundred and forty statements were selected for try out of tool.

III. Try-out of the Tool

The duplicated try-out tool in Oriya was given with an instruction for responding the items in consultation with language experts for language difficulty and clear understanding. The statements in each area were presented separately. The tool was administered on 60 students and collected. The students were to rate each statement and on a three point scale viz. "agree, indifferent and disagree" No time limit was fixed for responding the scale.

IV. Selection

The try-out tool was scored on the basis of agreement score, i.e. 3, 2 and 1 were awarded for agree, indifferent and disagree respectively. The items were selected on the basis of discriminating power by using the following formula.

$$D.P. = \frac{U - L}{N} \times 100$$

To identify the upper and lower group the tryout tools were arranged in high to low order on the basis of score. Then the top 33 per cent and bottom 33 per cent were taken as upper and lower group respectively.

The value of discriminating power in each area were arranged from high to low order and five statements from highest positive values and five statements from highest negative values were selected. So in all 40 statements were selected.

V. Final Tool

The selected items were edited randomly. The edited tool was having provision to indicate biodata at the top followed by necessary instructions. Then the 10 carbon copies of the tool were administered on 10 students to verify case of responding. Then the tool was printed. The printed tool is given in Appendix—C.

Items for each of the four dimensions of attitude were selected on the basis of significance of 't' ratios. Items for attitude towards school (i.e. 10 items), attitude towards teachers (i.e. 10 items), attitude towards classmates (i.e. 10 items) and attitude towards curriculum (i.e. 10 items), a total of 40 items were selected for final scale. The items under each of the four headings and their corresponding 't' value are presented in Table 3.5.

VI. Scoring Procedure

The weightages 3, 2 and 1 were assigned to agree, indifferent and disagree scale points of favourable statements respectively and 1, 2, 3 were assigned to agree, indifferent and disagree scale points of unfavourable statements respectively.

The area-wise serial numbers of favourable and unfavourable recorded statements in the final scale were recorded as per the following table to obtain area-wise score and to facilitate scoring.

Table 3.5: 't' Ratios of 40 Items under four Aspects of Attitude

Item	*'t' ratio*	*Item*	*'t' ratio*	*Item*	*'t' ratio*	*Item*	*'t' ratio*
school		*teacher*		*classmate*		*curriculum*	
1	8.31	11	2.99	21	4.31	31	4.72
2	5.43	12	3.21	22	6.11	32	5.93
3	4.94	13	4.53	23	2.93	33	7.25
4	4.56	14	2.93	24	8.74	34	3.91
5	3.96	15	5.31	25	5.79	35	4.74
6	4.62	16	7.34	26	6.73	36	3.53
7	3.97	17	3.61	27	5.81	37	4.59
8	6.43	18	7.30	28	6.25	38	3.78
9	6.02	19	2.98	29	3.88	39	3.62
10	3.91	20	6.41	30	4.95	40	8.70

Table 3.6: Area-wise Serial Number of Favourable and Unfavourable Statements in the Final Scale

Attitude area	*Serial no. of statements*	
	Favourable	*Unfavourable*
School	1, 2, 3, 6, 8, 9, 10	4, 5, 7
Teacher	11, 12, 13, 14, 17, 18, 20	15, 16, 19
Classmates	21, 24, 26, 27, 28	22, 23, 25, 29, 30
Curriculum	32, 34, 36, 37, 38	31, 33, 35, 39, 40

EVALUATION OF THE SCALE

The reliability and validity of the tool were borne by the following methods:

I. Test-retest Method of Reliability

The determination of stability is important for this type of tool which was determined by this method. The scale was administered twice on random sample of 100 students of four randomly selected high schools at a gap of 15 days. The scales were scored to get two sets of scores on four attitude area and scale as a whole (Table 3.7)

Table 3.7: Reliability Co-efficient of Sub-scales and Scale as a Whole of Attitude Scale by Test-retest Method

Reliability coefficient	*Sub Scales*				
	School	*Teacher*	*Classmates*	*Curriculum*	*Wholescale*
	.75	.78	.82	.77	.78

All the reliability coefficients were significant beyond .01 which indicate high reliability of the scale.

II. Validity of the Scale

The validity of the scale was borne out by the following method:

Content Validity

In constructing the tool the statements were collected from the students, literature and experts. This method of collection of items prove the inclusiveness of universe of the concepts and contents. This indicates high content validity of the scale.

Face Validity

The original list of 140 statements were scrutinised by the panel of experts. Then one hundred statements were tried out on 60 students. Then each item was analysed to determine how efficiently it differentiated between the upper and lower 33 per cent of the individual in the distribution of scores. Only these items which clearly discriminate between two groups were included. This type of inclusion of items in scale proves the high face validity of the scale.

Concurrent Validity

In order to determine the concurrent validity of the scale three teachers from four sample schools were selected randomly. They were asked to name ten poorly adjusted and ten well adjusted students from class X of their school. In poorly adjusted group they were instructed to include students who dislike school, teacher, classmate and curriculum. In well adjusted group they were asked to include students who have likeness towards these areas. The attitude scale then was administered on these two groups. The scores on the sub-scales of the two groups were compared. It showed a significant agreement between the judgement of teachers and the scores on the scales. This evidences the high concurrent validity of the scale.

The above discussions indicate the high reliability and validity of the scale. The evaluated scale was then ready for collection of data and further use.

Occupational Aspiration Scale (OAS)

The Haller and Miller's Occupational Aspiration Scale adopted in Indian situation by J.S. Grewal in 1984 was used in the present study (i.e. to verify H 1.7.4). The original test was in English version and consists of a 8 multiple choice items having 10 alternatives in each item. The scale asks for both short and long range realistic as well as idealistic expressions of the level of occupational preferences. The scale is self administering and can be used individually as well as in groups. There is no time limit but half an hour is sufficient for the administration of the test. Responses are scored 'zero' through 'nine'. The total score is the sum of the scores for each of the eight items which can range from '0' to '72'. The scale has been validated against Haller and Miller's Occupational Aspiration Scale and the validity coefficient has been reported to be 0.75 by the author. Reliability coefficients by test-retest method and by spilt-half method are reported to be 0.84 and 0.54 respectively.

All the eight items were scored in a uniform pattern given in the manual of the test. The total score on eight items was taken as the individual's occupational aspiration score.

Copies of the scale and the scoring key are given in Appendices D and D-1 respectively.

Educational Aspiration Scale (from-P) (EAS)

Educational Aspiration Scale (EAS) for-P, prepared by Sharma and Gupta (1980) and translated into Oriya by Mishra (1990) is specifically designed for secondary school pupils (i.e. to verify H 1.7.5). It is based on paired comparison technique and consisted of 45 items. It is a self-explanatory scale and can be administered individually and in groups. There is no time limit, however it takes about 25 minutes to administer the whole scale. The responses are scored as '1' to '0'. The total score, which ranges from '0' to '45' determines an individual's standing on the scale. The coefficients of reliability by test-retest method (stability) and split half method (internal consistency) have been reported to be .980 and .903 in the manual of the scale. Validity coefficient against scholastic Achievement is reported to be .692 and the predictive validity with EAS (form-V) is reported to be .596.

All the forty-five items were scored according to the scoring key provided in the manual of the test. The total score determined the standing of the individual on the scale.

Achievement Motivation Inventory

Achievement Motivation Inventory standardized by Mehta (1969) was used in this study (i.e. to verify H 1.7.6). The inventory is meant for high school students. The inventory contains 22 items with six alternatives of which the respondents are required to check one. In each item out of six responses two are related to achievement (AR), two are related task (TR) and two are unrelated to achievement (UR). The numbers given against each item under AR, TR and UR in the scoring key show the nature of the numbered responses. For example response numbers 2 and 5 out of six responses under item 1 and

AR responses to item 1 and responses number 1 and 4 are TR responses and responses 3 and 6 are UR responses. The response to any one item can be either AR or TR or UR. The students took 30 minutes to complete the inventory which has also been suggested by the author.

The K-R-20 reliability of the inventory was 0.67 and split half reliability was found 0.55. Theoretical validation of the AMI has been presented by the test author.

Achievement Score

No specific test was used to assess the academic achievement of the subjects by the investigator. It was decided to take the total marks secured by the subjects in the Annual H.S.C. examinations for the three sessions (i.e. 1996-97, 1997-98 and 1998-99) conducted by the Board of Secondary Education, Orissa for the purpose. Accordingly the results of the said examinations (i.e. division-wise and pass-fail-wise) were collected from the five randomly chosen Ashram Schools and five randomly chosen Education Department High Schools out of the sampled schools through their headmasters/ headmistresses for the three sessions (i.e. 1996-97, 1997-98 and 98-99).

COLLECTION OF DATA

For the collection of data from the sample Ashram Schools and Non-Ashram Schools, necessary permission of District Welfare Officers and Circle Inspectors of Schools was sought. The heads of the selected schools were contacted on the spot. The task of data collection was accomplished in three phases: the first phase comprised collection of data pertaining to the assessment of socio-economic status, attitude, occupational aspiration, educational aspiration and achievement motivation of the students. The tests were administered to the sample students of grade X of the sample schools present on the day of data collection. The students, who were not selected, were asked to go to another room where they were attended by their teachers. All the five tests were administered systematically in a proper sequence in two sessions of a day, having a break of half an hour, of maximum three hours.

Before giving the tests to the subjects efforts were made to establish rapport with the students followed by a motivation talk regarding general purposes of psychological testing for the students. The basic purpose of the present study was, however, not disclosed to the subjects. The subjects were asked to fill up the identification data at the top of the answer sheet. Separate standard instructions were given to the students as given in the manuals of the tests. As there was no time limit for any of the tests (except the Achievement Motivation Inventory), the students were asked to respond to each item of the tests and to proceed to the next item as soon as they completed one. Before permitting the subjects to answer, their doubts were clarified and they were given freedom to get clarified their doubts while taking the tests. The second phase of data collection aimed at studying the school's facilities. As such the data were collected from the twenty five headmasters/headmistresses of the sample schools (i.e. 13 Ashram Schools and 12 Education Department High Schools). The third phase involves collection of achievement scores of the sample students. After the publication of the results of B.S.E., 1999, Orissa in the month of June the total marks secured by the sample students were collected from the schools through the heads of the institutions.

Scoring of the tools was done in accordance with the procedures stipulated for each of them in the respective manuals. The scores of all the subjects on socio-economic status, attitudes, occupational aspiration, educational aspiration, achievement motivation and achievement are given in Appendix (G-1 and 2). After scoring all the tests, the investigator organized the whole data, checked it to see the accuracy utility and completeness. After editing, the data were classified and tabulated for its analysis according to the objectives of the study.

Statistical Techniques Used

The following statistical techniques were employed as per the design of the study for testing of various hypotheses.

- Chi–square (x^2)
- CR/'t' test

Analysis and Interpretation of Data

In the present chapter analysis, interpretation and presentation of results have been provided systematically. In the present investigation, an attempt has been made to evaluate the Ashram High Schools in Orissa in respect of student achievement. The design and methodology employed for conducting the study have been discussed in the preceding chapter. The data were got analysed through appropriate statistical techniques. The results were interpreted in terms of the relevant objectives and hypotheses formulated for the study, which follows in the following sections.

TESTING HYPOTHESIS ONE

In pursuance of the objective 1 of the study (i.e. 1.6.1) the first null hypothesis (i.e. 1.7.1) was formulated which states that there will be no significant difference in socio-economic status between the students of Ashram and Education Department High Schools. For the purpose of testing the above null hypothesis, 2x2 contingency table was prepared and the chi-square test (x^2) of independence was applied either to accept or to reject the null hypothesis. In order to have two groups of high socio-economic status and low socio-economic status students (in both Ashram and Education Department High School) demonstrating their respective peculiarities, P75 and P25 were calculated respectively. For the purpose the distribution of SES scores for the total group of students is reflected in Table 4.1.

Table 4.1: Distribution of SES Scores of Total Students

CI	*F*	*Cf*	
190-199	3	1000	
180-189	7	997	
170-179	5	990	
160-169	8	985	
150-159	11	977	
140-149	12	966	
130-139	15	954	
120-129	31	939	
110-119	30	908	
100-109	52	878	
90-99	40	826	
80-89	58	786	
70-79	72	728	P_{75} = 83.29 or 83
60-69	78	656	
50-59	100	578	
40-49	113	478	P_{25} = 32.49 or 32
30-39	164	365	
20-29	147	201	
10-19	54	54	

A reference to Table 4.1 reveals that the P_{75} and P_{25} values are 83 and 32 respectively. On the basis of this, it can be said that a student who scores 83 or more belongs to high socio-economic status group, whereas a student who scores 32 or less belongs to low socio-economic status group. On the basis of these two way classification the number of students belonging to Ashram and Education Department High Schools was decided and was used for statistical treatment. The result of chi-square test has been presented in Table 4.2.

Table 4.2 indicates that the chi-square value of 195.64 with df 1 is significant at 0.01 level of significance. It suggests that both the group of students (i.e. Ashram and Education

Table 4.2: Chi-square Results on SES Scores of Compared Groups (i.e. Ashram vs. Education Department High School Students)

Groups for comparison	*A+C*	*B+D*
HSES	43	210
LSES	188	256

$X^2 = 195.64$, $P<.01$

HSES = High socio-economic status

LSES = Low socio-economic status.

A = SC/ST students of Ashram Schools

B = SC/ST students of Education Department High Schools

C = Non-SC/ST students of Ashram High Schools

D = Non-SC/ST students of Education Department High schools

Department High Schools) significantly differ with regard to their socio-economic status. Hence the null hypothesis (i.e. 1.7.1) of no significant difference in socio-economic status between the students of Ashram and Education Department High Schools was rejected. Further an examination of frequencies of respective cells in the contingency table indicates that the number of students belonging to the Education Department high schools in the high socio-economic status group was relatively higher than those of the Ashram High Schools. So it can be concluded that the students of Education Department High Schools were from higher socio-economic status in comparison to their Ashram High School students counterparts.

A further cross analysis of various group combinations between SES and school has been undertaken. In this connection various sub-hypotheses were formulated for testing. Each sub-hypothesis has been tested with the help of chi-square test.

Sub-hypothesis 1.1

There will be no significant difference in the distributions of socio-economic status scores between the SC/

ST students of Ashram High Schools and the SC/ST students of Education Department High Schools. To test this null hypothesis, chi-square test was applied. The result is given in Table 4.3.

Table 4.3: Chi-square Value for the SC/ST Students of Ashram and Education Department High Schools and SES Scores

Groups for comparison	*A*	*B*
HSES	21	10
LSES	177	19

$X^2 = 12.23, P<.01$

The critical value of chi-square with df 1 at .01 level is 6.635. The observed value of chi-square (vide Table 4.3) is significant. Hence the data provide enough evidence that the SC/ST students of Ashram High Schools and the SC/ST students of Education Department High Schools differ significantly on the basis of their socio-economic status. So, the null hypothesis (i.e. 1.1) was rejected. An examination of table values indicates that the number of SC/ST students belonging to the Education Department High Schools in the low socio-economic status group was relatively lesser than those of the Ashram High Schools in the same group. Thus it can be said that SC/ST students of Education Department High Schools were from higher socio-economic status as compared to the SC/ST students of Ashram High Schools.

Sub-hypothesis 1.2

There will be no significant difference in the distributions of socio-economic status scores between the SC/ST students and the non-SC/ST students of Ashram High Schools. The result of chi-square is given in Table 4.4.

Table 4.4 shows that there is significant difference in the socio-economic status between the SC/ST students and the non-SC/ST students of Ashram High Schools. Thus the above stated null-hypothesis (i.e. 1.2) is rejected. It may be said on the basis of the above table values, that the non-SC/

Table 4.4: Chi-square Value for the SC/ST Students and non-SC/ST Students of Ashram High Schools on SES Scores

Groups for comparison	*A*	*C*
HSES	21	22
LSES	177	11

$X^2 = 58.68$, $P<.01$

ST students of Ashram High Schools were from higher socio-economic status as compared to their SC/ST counterparts.

Sub-hypothesis 1.3

There will be no significant difference in the distributions of socio-economic status scores between the SC/ST students of Ashram High Schools and the non-SC/ST students of Education Department High Schools.

Table 4.5: Chi-square value for the SC/ST Students of Ashram High Schools and non-SC/ST Students of Education Department High Schools

Groups for comparison	*A*	*D*
HSES	21	200
LSES	177	27

$X^2 = 254.48$, $P<.01$

It is indicated from Table 4.5 that there is significant difference in the socio-economic status between the SC/ST students of Ashram High Schools and the non-SC/ST students of Education Department High Schools. The above stated null-hypothesis is rejected. The table reveals that the non-SC/ST students of Education Department High Schools were from higher socio-economic status in comparison to their SC/ST counterparts of Ashram Schools.

Sub-hypothesis 1.4

There will be no significant difference in the distributions of socio-economic status scores between the SC/

ST students of Education Department High Schools and the non-SC/ST students of Ashram High Schools.

Table 4.6: Chi-square Value for the SC/ST Students of Education Department High Schools and non-SC/ST Students of Ashram High Schools on SES Scores

Groups for comparison	*B*	*C*
HSES	10	22
LSES	19	11

$X^2 = 6.4, P<.05$

Table 4.6 illustrates that the chi-square value comes out to be 6.4 which is significant at .05 level; thus null hypothesis is rejected. This implies that the Socio-economic status of the SC/ST students of Education Department High Schools and the non-SC/ST students of Ashram High Schools differ significantly. The data in the above table suggest that the non-SC/ST students of Ashram High Schools were from higher socio-economic status in comparison to the SC/ST students of Education Department High Schools.

Sub-hypothesis 1.5

There will be no significant difference in the distributions of socio-economic status scores between the SC/ST students and the non-SC/ST students of Education Department High Schools on SES scores.

Table 4.7: Chi-square Value for the SC/ST Students and the Non-SC/ST Students of Education Department High Schools on SES Scores

Groups for comparison	*B*	*D*
HSES	10	200
LSES	19	27

$X^2 = 50.16, P<.01$

From the chi-square value (vide Table 4.7) it is quite obvious that the number of non-SC/ST students of Education

Department High Schools in the high socio-economic status group was relatively higher than those of the SC/ST students of Education Department High Schools. Thus, it can be said that the non-SC/ST students of Education Department High Schools were from higher socio-economic status as compared to their SC/ST student counterparts. On the basis of this result the null hypothesis (i.e. 1.5) was rejected.

Sub-hypothesis 1.6

There will be no significant difference in the distributions of socio-economic status scores of the non-SC/ST students of Ashram Schools and the non-SC/ST students of Education Department High Schools on SES Scores.

To test this null hypothesis chi-square test was applied and the result is given in Table 4.8

Table 4.8: Chi-square Value for the Non-SC/ST Students of Ashram High Schools and the Non-SC/ST Students of Education Department High Schools

Groups for comparison	*C*	*D*
HSES	22	200
LSES	11	27

$X^2 = 10.61$, $P<.01$

The chi-square value as reported by the table (vide Table 4.8, $X^2 = 10.61$, $P<.01$) is significant which implies that the non SC/ST students of Ashram High Schools and the non-SC/ST students of Education Department High Schools differ significantly in their socio-economic status. Hence the null hypothesis was rejected. It may further be interpreted on the basis of the cell values that the non-SC/ST students of Education Department High Schools were from higher socio-economic status in comparison to the non-SC/ST students of Ashram High Schools.

Sub-hypothesis 1.7

There will be no significant difference in the distributions of socio-economic status scores of the SC/ST students and non-SC/ST students on SES scores.

Chi-square test was applied to test this null hypothesis and the result is given in Table 4.9.

Table 4.9: Chi-square Value for the SC/ST Students and the Non-SC/ST Students on SES Scores

Groups for comparison	*A+B*	*C+D*
HSES	31	222
LSES	196	38

$X^2 = 24.98$, $P<.01$

Table 4.9 indicates that there is significant difference in the socio-economic status between the SC/ST students and the non-SC/ST students. This leads to assert that the SC/ST students and the non-SC/ST students differ significantly with regard to their socio-economic status. Hence the null hypothesis (i.e. 1.7) was rejected. On the basis of the frequencies of respective cells in the contingency table, it can be interpreted that the non-SC/ST students were from higher socio-economic status group than their SC/ST counterparts.

TESTING HYPOTHESIS TWO

The second objective of the study was to evaluate the facilities of Ashram High Schools taking Education Department High Schools as parameter. Hence the second corresponding null hypothesis was as follows:

"There will be no significant difference in the mean scores on different facility areas of Ashram High Schools and Education Department High Schools".

In this connection relevant data were collected from the twenty five headmasters/headmistresses of Ashram High Schools and twenty five headmasters/headmistresses of Education Department High Schools with the help of Secondary School Facilities Survey Questionnaire (SSFSQ) which was developed by the investigator. The SSFSQ consists of thirteen items. The item wise scores were arranged separately for statistical treatment for those two types of school. To verify the null hypothesis (i.e. 1.7.2) 't'-test was applied. The summary of the results is given in Table 4.10.

Table 4.10: Comparison of Facilities of Ashram High Schools and Education Department High Schools through 't'-test

Items		*Facilities*	*Group*	*M*	*'t'-value*
1		School Building	AS	3.4	0.73
			EDS	3.0	
2		Space	AS	20.6	3.79**
			EDS	14.6	
3		Furniture	AS	19.6	1.04
			EDS	18.0	
4		Inside space	AS	10.2	0.54
			EDS	9.8	
5	*(i)*	General Teaching Aids	AS	9.0	0.94
			EDS	10.9	
	(ii)	Science Teaching Aids	AS	9.3	0.47
			EDS	8.5	
	(iii)	Social Study Teaching Aids	AS	7.2	0.64
			EDS	6.7	
6		Equipment	AS	6.8	2.14*
			EDS	8.88	
7		Audio-visual Aids	AS	1.0	0.54
			EDS	1.3	
8		Subject Teachers	AS	12.7	4.86**
			EDS	10.0	
9		Common Facilities	AS	4.2	0.89
			EDS	3.5	
10		Hostel	AS	3.0	2.24*
			EDS	1.3	
11		Tutorial Arrangement	AS	2.7	2.11*
			EDS	0.9	
12	*(i)*	Student-Teacher ratio	AS	9.0	2.18*
			EDS	6.0	
	(ii)	Student Non-Teaching personnel ratio	AS	9.0	2.15*
			EDS	6.0	
13		Land	AS	10.0	2.4*
			EDS	7.4	

*P<.05

**P<.01

AS = Ashram High School

EDS = Education Department High Schools

It may be seen from Table 4.10 that there were significant differences in facilities related to the areas of space ($t=3.79$, $P<.01$), equipment ($t=2.14$, $P<.05$), subject teachers ($t=4.86$ $P<.01$) hostel ($t=2.24$, $P<.05$), tutorial arrangement ($t=2.11$, $P<.05$), student teacher ratio ($t=2.18$, $P<.05$), student – non-teaching personnel ratio ($t=2.15$, $P<.05$) and land ($t=2.40$, $P<.05$) between Ashram High Schools and Education Department High Schools. All the mean differences (excepting equipment) were in favour of Ashram Schools. In case of other facilities, i.e. school building, furniture, inside space, science teaching aids, social study teaching aids, common facilities (excepting general teaching aids and audio-visual aids) where the differences were in favour of Education Department High Schools though differences were not significant, the differences were in favour of Ashram High Schools. The superiority of Education Department High Schools were marked only in case of equipment. Hence the null hypothesis (i.e. 1.7.2) was partly accepted and partly rejected.

TESTING HYPOTHESIS THREE

The null hypothesis three (i.e. 1.7.3) states that there will be no significant differences in the distributions of performance at the Annual H.S.C. examination between:

1. The SC/ST students and the non-SC/ST students of Ashram High Schools.
2. The SC/ST students and non-SC/ST students of Education Department High Schools.
3. The SC/ST students of Ashram High Schools and the SC/ST students of Education Department High Schools.
4. The SC/ST students and the non-SC/ST students.
5. The Ashram High School students and the Education Department High School students.

For this purpose 05 Ashram High Schools and 05 Education Department High Schools were randomly chosen from the sample schools. In this connection the division-wise

Table 4.11: Summary of Comparison of Annual H.S.C. Examination Results

Division	Frequency distributions								X2 of compared groups				
	SC/ST students		Non-SC/ST students		Total no. of SC/ST stduents A+B	Total no. of non-SC/ST students C+D	Total no. of AS stduents A+C	Total no. of EDHS students B+D	A vs. C	B vs. D	A vs. B	A+B vs. C+D	A+C vs. B+D
	AS(A)	EDH(B)	AS(C)	EDHS(D)									
1st	10	8	24	90	18	114	34	98	91.01**	23.21**	6.42 (N.S.)	60.15**	19.16**
2nd	36	19	57	113	55	170	93	132					
3rd	134	39	40	420	173	460	174	459					
Fail	114	48	15	185	162	200	129	233					
N	294	114	136	808	408	944	430	922					

*P<.05, **P<.01, N.S. = not significant, Remarks C>A; D>B; C+D>A+B; B+D>A+C

Annual H.S.C examination results of these two types of sample schools (i.e. 05 schools from each type) for three sessions, namely 1996-97, 1997-98, and 1998-99 were studied.

To test the above null hypothesis 4 x 2 contingency tables were prepared and the chi-square test of independence was applied either to accept or to reject the null hypothesis. The results of chi-square have been summarized in Table 4.11.

From Table 4.11 the overall picture that emerges from the chi-square test results shows that there were significant differences in the distributions of performance at the Annual H.S.C. examination between the SC/ST students and non-SC/ST students of Ashram High Schools (X^2 = 91.01, df-3, $P<.01$); between the SC/ST students and non-SC/ST students of Education Department High Schools (X^2 = 23.21, df-3, $P<.01$); between the SC/ST students and non-SC/ST students (X^2 = 60.15, $P<.01$) and between the Ashram High School and Education Department High School students (X^2 = 19.06, $P<.01$). Here the null hypothesis 1.7.3. (i, ii, iv and v) was rejected. However, significant differences were not noted in the distributions of performance at the Annual H.S.C. examination between the SC/ST students of Ashram High Schools and Education Department High Schools. Here the null hypothesis 1.7.3 (iii) was retained. On the basis of the weightage in the first and second division and weightage in the pass category, it can be said that the non-SC/ST students of Ashram High Schools performed better than the SC/ST students in the same schools. The non-SC/ST students of Education Department High Schools performed better than their SC/ST counterparts. The non-SC/ST students performed better than the SC/ST students as a whole. The students of Education Department High Schools performed better than the students of Ashram High Schools in the annual HSC. Examination.

TESTING HYPOTHESIS FOUR

This null hypothesis (i.e. 1.7.4) maintains that there will be no significant differences in mean scores of attitude towards school, teacher, classmates, and curriculum between:

1. The SC/ST students and the non-SC/ST students of Ashram Schools.

2. The SC/ST students and the non-SC/ST students of Education Department High Schools.

3. The SC/ST students of Ashram High Schools and the SC/ST students of Education Department High Schools;

4. The SC/ST students and the non-SC/ST students; and

5. The Ashram High School students and the Education Department High School students.

To verify this null hypothesis 't'-test was applied and the results are given in Table 4.12

A close perusal of Table 4.12 reveals that the SC/ST students of Ashram High Schools and the SC/ST students of Education Department High Schools ($t = 2.92$, $P<.01$) and the students of Ashram High Schools and Education Department High Schools ($t = 2.04$, $P<.05$) differed significantly in their attitude towards school. On the basis of the mean scores it can be said that the non SC/ST students were having more favourable attitude towards school than the SC/ST students of Ashram High Schools. Similarly the students of Education Department High Schools taken together were having more favourable attitude towards school than their Ashram High School counterparts.

When the attitude of the students of Ashram High Schools and Education Department High Schools towards curriculum was compared, it was found that the students of Education Department High Schools ($M = 26.55$) were having more favourable attitude towards curriculum ($t = 2.31$, $P<.05$). The rest of the t-values were not significant among the different groups for comparison. This implies that the various groups for comparison were having more or less same attitude towards curriculum. However, the various groups for comparison did not differ significantly in the attitude areas like attitude towards teacher and attitude towards classmates which indicate that the various groups for comparison were

Table 4.12: Significance of Differences in Mean Attitude Scores of Students of Ashram Schools and Education Department High Schools

Groups for comparison	*School*			*Teacher*			*Classmates*			*Curriculum*		
	N	*M*	*t-value*	*N*	*M*	*t-value*	*N*	*M*	*t-value*	*N*	*M*	*t-value*
A	468	23.98	2.92**	-	27.2	0.71	-	23.67	0.31	-	20.4	0.96
B	58	26.93		-	26.4		-	24.5		-	21.6	
B	58	26.93	0.21	-	26.4	0.01	-	24.5	0.29	-	21.6	1.21
D	412	26.16		-	26.5		-	23.8		-	23.7	
A	468	23.98	0.73	-	27.2	0.0	-	23.67	0.74	-	20.4	.63
C	62	25.0		-	27.2		-	25.01		-	21.2	
A+B	526	24.48	0.94	-	26.8	.00	-	24.08	0.19	-	21.2	1.04
C+D	474	25.58		-	26.85		-	24.41		-	22.45	
A+C	530	24.02	2.04*	-	27.21	0.34	-	24.34	0.05	-	20.8	2.31*
B+D	470	26.55		-	26.45		-	24.15		-	23.6	

*P<.05

**P<.01

having more or less same attitude towards teacher and classmates. In view of the results the null hypothesis was partly accepted and partly rejected.

TESTING HYPOTHESIS FIVE

This null hypothesis states that there will be no significant differences in the distributions of the level of occupational aspiration between:

1. The SC/ST students and the non-SC/ST students of Ashram High Schools;
2. The SC/ST students and the non-SC/ST students of Education Department High Schools;
3. The SC/ST students of Ashram High Schools and the SC/ST students of Education Department High Schools;
4. The SC/ST students and the non-SC/ST students; and
5. The students of Ashram High Schools and Education Department High Schools.

To test the above null hypothesis 2x2 contingency tables were prepared and the Chi-square test of independence was applied either to accept or to reject the null hypothesis. The results of Chi-square have been summarized in Table 4.13.

From Table 4.13 it can been seen that all the obtained Chi-square values [except for the SC/ST students of Ashram High Schools (i.e. A) Vs. the non-SC/ST students of Ashram High Schools (i.e. C); and for the SC/ST students of Ashram High Schools (i.e. A) Vs. the SC/ST students of Education Department High Schools (i.e. B)] were found significant. Thus it can be said that there were significant differences in the distributions of the level of occupational aspiration between the SC/ST students and non-SC/ST students of Education Department High Schools (x^2 = 10.90, df.1, P<.01); between the SC/ST students and non-SC/ST students (x^2 = 38.48, df.1, P<.01), and between the students of Ashram High Schools and Education Department High Schools (x^2 = 25.69, df.1, P<.01). Here the null hypothesis 1.7.5 (ii, iv and v) was rejected.

Table 4.13: Summary of Chi-square Results on Occupational Aspiration of Compared Groups

Level of O. Aspiration	*Frequency Distributions*								X^2 *of compared groups*				
	A	B	C	D	A+B	C+D	A+C	B+D	A vs C	B vs D	A vs B	A+B vs C+D	A+C vs B+D
High	78	11	14	146	89	160	92	157	3.43	10.90**	0.048	38.48**	25.69**
Low	143	22	12	84	165	96	155	106					

**P<.01

However, significant differences were not noted in the distributions of the level of occupational aspiration between the SC/ST students and non-SC/ST students of Ashram High Schools; and between the SC/ST students of Ashram and Education Department High Schools which indicate identical level of occupational aspiration. Hence the null hypothesis 1.7.5 (i and iii) were retained.

Looking to the frequency distributions in Table 4.13 the result indicates that the number of non-SC/ST students of Education Department High Schools in the high level of occupational aspiration group was relatively higher than those of the SC/ST students in the same schools. It tends to mean that the non-SC/ST students of Education Department High Schools were having higher level of occupational aspiration in comparison to their SC/ST counterparts. Similarly, the non-SC/ST students as a whole were having higher level of occupational aspiration as compared to their SC/ST counterparts. Further, the students of Education Department High Schools were having higher level of occupational aspiration than their Ashram counterparts.

TESTING HYPOTHESIS SIX

This null hypothesis states that there will be no significant differences in the distributions of the level of Educational aspiration between:

1. The SC/ST students and the non-SC/ST students of Ashram High Schools;
2. The SC/ST students and the non-SC/ST students of Education Department High Schools;
3. The SC/ST students of Ashram High Schools and the SC/ST students of Education Department High Schools;
4. The SC/ST students and the non-SC/ST students; and
5. The students of Ashram High Schools and Education Department High Schools.

To test the above null hypothesis chi-square test was applied, the results of which are summarised in Table 4.14.

Table 4.14: Summary of Chi-square Results on Educational Aspiration of Compared Groups

Level of E. Aspiration	*Frequency Distributions*								*X^2 of compared groups*				
	A	B	C	D	A+B	C+D	A+C	B+D	A vs C	B vs D	A vs B	A+B vs C+D	A+C vs B+D
High	151	19	18	109	170	127	169	128	2.41	1.16	0.118	3.88*	0.091
Low	109	12	22	105	121	127	131	117					

**P<.05

Table 4.14 indicates that out of five values of Chi-square, only one value was found to be significant (x^2 = 3.88, df.1, P<.05 for A+B Vs. C+D). It suggests significant difference in the distribution of the level of educational aspiration between the SC/ST students and non-SC/ST students. Here the null hypothesis 1.7.6 (iv) was rejected. An examination of frequencies of respective cells in the contingency table indicates that the number of SC/ST students in the category of high level of educational aspiration was relatively higher than their non-SC/ST counterparts. It implies that the SC/ ST students had significantly higher level of educational aspiration than their non-SC/ST counterparts. The other four pairs of group, however, occupied the similar position in their level of educational aspiration. Hence the null hypothesis (i.e. 1.7.6-i, ii, iii and v) was retained.

TESTING HYPOTHESIS SEVEN

This null hypothesis (i.e. 1.7.7) states that there will be no significant differences in mean scores of achievement motivation between:

1. The SC/ST students and the non SC/ST students of Ashram High Schools;
2. The SC/ST students and the non-SC/ST students of Education Department High Schools;
3. The SC/ST students of Ashram High Schools and the SC/ST students of Education Department High Schools;
4. The SC/ST students and the non-SC/ST students; and
5. The students of Ashram High Schools and Educatio1 Department High Schools.

In order to test the null hypothesis, the mean achievement motivation scores of the various groups were calculated and 't' test was used to examine the significance of difference between the two means. The relevant results are presented in Table 4.15.

Table 4.15: Significance of Difference in Mean Achievement Motivation Scores of Students of Ashram High Schools and Education Department High Schools

Groups for comparison	*N*	*M*	*S.D*	*t-value*
A	468	4.8	1.85	2.68**
C	62	5.9	3.14	
B	58	5.3	3.37	5.92**
D	412	8.2	4.43	
A	468	4.8	1.85	1.11
B	58	5.3	3.37	
A+B	526	5.03	2.60	9.57**
C+D	474	7.04	3.76	
A+C	530	5.35	2.50	6.67**
B+D	470	6.75	3.90	

**P<.01

It may be observed from Table 4.15 that there were significant differences in mean achievement motivation scores between the SC/ST students and non-SC/ST students of Ashram High Schools (t=2.68, P<.01), between the SC/ST students and the non-SC/ST students of Education Department High Schools (t=5.92, P<.01); between the SC/ST students and the non-SC/ST students (t=9.57, P<.01), and between the students of Ashram and Education Department High Schools (t=6.67, P<.01). Hence the null hypothesis was rejected here. On the basis of the mean scores, it can be said that the non-SC/ST students of Ashram High Schools were having more n-Ach than their SC/ST counterparts. Further, the non-SC/ST students of Education Department High Schools appeared to have greater magnitude of n-Ach in comparison to the SC/ST students in the same schools. The non-SC/ST students showed superiority over SC/ST students with reference to n-Ach. It can also be seen (vide Table 4.15) that the students of Education Department High Schools had significantly higher n-Ach than the students of Ashram High Schools.

However, no significant difference was noticed in the distributions of the n-Ach between the SC/ST students of Ashram High Schools and the SC/ST students of Education Department High Schools which indicates that both the groups of students occupied the similar position in their n-Ach. Hence the null hypothesis (i.e. 1.7.7-3) was retained.

5

Summary and Conclusions

INTRODUCTION

In pursuance of the directives of the Indian constitutions and the special provisions made therein for the SC/ST, the Government of India has been implementing special programmes for the social, economic and educational development of these tribal groups. The major objectives of these programmes have been to develop these aboriginals in the direction of modernity so as to enable them to secure for themselves an equitable and rightful place in the national system. From time to time various provisions have been made to uplift the SC/STs. One such provision is the establishment of Ashram schools. These schools have been set up to bring up the disadvantaged children at par with other category of children. Here a question comes to our mind, "How far these schools are successful to uplift the SC/ST students to the level of other category of students?"

In order to answer the above question a systematic inquiry is highly essential to evaluate this type of school.

OBJECTIVES

The study was carried out keeping the following objectives in view:

1. To investigate the socio-economic background of the students of Ashram High Schools in comparison to Education Department High Schools.

2. To evaluate the facilities of Ashram High Schools taking Education Department High Schools as parameters.

3. To evaluate the performance of students of Ashram High School with reference to students of Education Department High Schools at the Annual H.S.C. examination.

4. To evaluate the attitude, level of occupational and educational aspirations and n-Ach of students of Ashram High Schools taking the students of Education Department High Schools as the parameter.

HYPOTHESES

Following null hypothesis have been formulated keeping the objectives in view:

1. There will be no significant difference in socio-economic status between the students of Ashram High Schools and Education Department High Schools.

2. There will be no significant difference in the mean scores on different facility areas of Ashram High Schools and Education Department High Schools.

3. There will be no significant difference in the distributions of performance at the Annual H.S.C. examination between:

   (i) the SC/ST students and the non SC/ST students of Ashram High Schools;

   (ii) the SC/ST students and the non SC/ST students of Education Department High Schools.

   (iii) The SC/ST students of Ashram High Schools and the SC/ST students of Education Department High Schools;

   (iv) The SC/ST students and the non SC/ST students; and

   (v) The students of Ashram High Schools and the students of Education Department High Schools.

4. There will be no significant differences in mean scores of attitude towards school, teacher, classmates and curriculum between:
   - *(i)* the SC/ST students and the non SC/ST students of Ashram High Schools;
   - *(ii)* the SC/ST students and the non SC/ST students of Education Department High Schools;
   - *(iii)* the SC/ST students of Ashram High Schools and the SC/ST students of Education Department High Schools;
   - *(iv)* the SC/ST students and the non SC/ST students; and
   - *(v)* the students of Ashram High Schools and the student of Education Department High Schools.
5. There will be no significant differences in the distributions of the level of occupational aspiration between:
   - *(i)* the SC/ST students and the non SC/ST students of High Schools;
   - *(ii)* the SC/ST students and the non SC/ST students of Education Department High Schools;
   - *(iii)* the SC/ST students of Ashram High Schools and the SC/ST students of Education Department High Schools;
   - *(iv)* the SC/ST students and the non SC/ST students; and
   - *(v)* the students of Ashram High Schools and the students of Education Department High Schools.
6. There will be no significant differences in the distributions of the level of education aspiration between:

(*i*) the SC/ST students and the non SC/ST students of Ashram High Schools;

(*ii*) the SC/ST students and the non SC/ST students of Educational Department High Schools;

(*iii*) the SC/ST students of Ashram High Schools and the SC/ST students of Education Department High Schools;

(*iv*) the SC/ST students and the non SC/ST students; and

(*v*) the students of Ashram High Schools and the students of Education Department High Schools.

7. There will be no significant differences in mean scores of achievement motivation between:

(*i*) the SC/ST students and the non SC/ST students of Ashram High Schools;

(*ii*) the SC/ST students and the non SC/ST students of Education Department High Schools;

(*iii*) the SC/ST students of Ashram High Schools and the SC/ST students of Education Department High Schools;

(*iv*) the SC/ST students and the non SC/ST students; and

(*v*) the students of Ashram High Schools and the students of Education Department High Schools.

STRATEGY OF INVESTIGATION

A representative sample of 1000 students, out of which 394 ST, 74 SC and 62 non-SC/ST students from Ashram High Schools; and 16 ST, 42 SC, and 412 non-SC/ST students from the Education Department High Schools were selected for this study. In order to compare the school facilities 13 heads of the Ashram High Schools and 12 heads of the Education Department High Schools were randomly chosen.

The following measuring devices were used to collect relevant data required for the study.

1. Socio-Economic Status Scale (Kamila, 1985)
2. Secondary School Facilities Scale, (Developed by the Investigator)
3. An Attitude Scale (Developed by the Investigator)
4. Occupational Aspiration Scale (Grewal, 1984).
5. Educational Aspiration Scale (Gupta, 1980).
6. Achievement Motivation Inventory (Mehta, 1969)
7. Result of student's performance at the Annual H.S.C. examination.

The data collected from the various sources were analysed using the Chi-square test and 't' test.

MAJOR FINDINGS

The preceding chapter has been devoted to the analysis and interpretation of data. The analyses have yielded some significant findings. Major findings have been presented under the following heads:

1. Findings pertaining to the socio-economic background of the students;
2. Findings pertaining to the facilities of the schools;
3. Findings pertaining to the performance of the students at the Annual H.S.C. examination;
4. Finding pertaining to the attitude of the students;
5. Findings pertaining to the level of occupational aspiration of the students;

6. Findings pertaining to the level of educational aspiration of the students; and

7. Findings pertaining to the achievement motivation of the students.

1. Findings Pertaining to the Socio-economic Background of the Students

(a) The students of Ashram and Education Department High Schools differed significantly with regard to their socio-economic status. The students of Education Department High Schools were having higher socio-economic background in comparison to the students of Ashram Schools.

(b) The SC/ST students of Education Department High Schools were from higher socio-economic status as compared to the SC/ST students of Ashram High Schools.

(c) When the SC/ST students and non-SC/ST students of Ashram High Schools were compared it was found that the non-SC/ST students were from higher socio-economic status.

(d) Significant difference was found between the SC/ST students of Ashram High Schools and the non-SC/ST students of Education Department High Schools in the socio-economic status.

(e) There was significant difference between the SC/ST students of Education Department High Schools and the non-SC/ST students of Ashram High Schools with respect to socio-economic status and the differences was in favour of the non-SC/ST students of Ashram High Schools.

(f) Striking difference was noticed in the socio-economic status of the non-SC/ST students and SC/ST students of Education Department High Schools and the difference was in favour of the non-SC/ST students.

(g) The non –SC/ST students of Ashram and Education Department High Schools differed significantly in their socio-economic status and the differences goes in favour of the non SC/ST students of Education Department High Schools.

(h) Significant difference existed in the socio-economic status of the SC/ST students and the non-SC/ST students. The non-SC/ST students were from higher socio-economic status than their SC/ST counterparts.

2 Findings Pertaining to the Facilities of the Schools

(a) There were significant differences in facilities related to the areas of space, equipment, subject teachers, hostel, tutorial arrangement, student-teacher ratio, student-non-teaching personnel ratio and land between the Ashram and Education Department High Schools. All the mean differences (excepting equipment) were in favour of Ashram High Schools. On the other hand the superiority of Education Department High Schools was marked only in case of facility related to the area of equipment.

(b) No significant differences were observed between the Ashram and the Education Department High Schools in the facility areas like school buildings, furniture, inside space, general teaching aids, Science teaching aids, social study teaching aids, audio visual aids, and common facilities.

3. Findings Pertaining to the Performance of the Students at the Annual H.S.C. Examination

(a) Significant differences were noted in the distribution of performance at the Annual H.S.C. examination between the SC/ST students and non-SC/ST students belonging to Ashram High Schools; between SC/ST students and non –SC/ST students of Education Department High Schools; between the SC/ST students and non-SC/ST students, and between the students of Ashram and Education Department High Schools.

(*b*) The SC/ST students of Ashram High Schools and Education Department High Schools did not differ significantly in the distributions of performance at the Annual H.S.C. examination.

(*c*) The non-SC/ST students of Ashram High Schools performed better than the SC/ST students in the same schools.

(*d*) The non-SC/ST students of Education Department High Schools performed better than their SC/ST counterparts.

(*e*) The non-SC/ST students as a whole performed better than the SC/ST students as a whole.

(*f*) The students of Education Department High Schools performed better than the students of Ashram High Schools in the Annual H.S.C. examination.

4. Findings Pertaining to the Attitude of the Students

(*a*) The SC/ST students of Ashram High Schools and the Education Department High Schools differed significantly in their attitude towards school and the difference was in favour of the SC/ST students of Education Department High Schools.

(*b*) The students of Education Department High Schools taken together were having more favourable attitude towards schools than their Ashram school counterparts.

(*c*) With respect to the attitude towards curriculum the students of Education Department High Schools were found to have more favourable attitude than the students of Ashram High Schools.

(*d*) The various groups for comparison did not differ significantly in their attitude towards teacher and classmates.

5. Findings Pertaining to the Level of Occupational Aspiration of the Students

(*a*) Significant differences were noted in the distributions of the level of occupational aspiration between the SC/ST students and non-SC/ST students of Education Department High Schools; between the SC/ST students and non-SC/ST students and between the students of Ashram High Schools and the Education Department High Schools.

(*b*) The non-SC/ST students of Education Department High Schools were having higher level of occupational aspiration in comparison to their SC/ST counterparts.

(*c*) The non-SC/ST students as a whole were having higher level of occupational aspiration as compared to their SC/ST counterparts.

(*d*) The students of Education Department High Schools were having higher level of occupational aspiration than their Ashram counterparts.

(*e*) No significant differences were found in the distributions of the level of occupational aspiration between the SC/ST students and non-SC/ST students of Ashram High Schools; and between the SC/ST students of Ashram and the Education Department High Schools.

6. Findings Pertaining to the Level of Educational Aspiration of the Students

(*a*) Significant difference in the distribution of the level of educational aspiration between the SC/ST and non-SC/ST students was observed and the difference was in favour of the SC/ST students.

(b) No significant differences were observed in the distributions of the level of educational aspiration between the SC/ST and non-SC/ST students of Ashram High Schools; between the SC/ST and non-SC/ST students of Education Department High Schools; between the SC/ST students of Ashram and Education Department High Schools; and between the students of Ashram and Education Department High Schools.

7. Findings Pertaining to the Achievement Motivation of the Students

(a) There were significant differences in mean achievement motivation scores between the SC/ST students and non-SC/ST students of Ashram High Schools; between the SC/ST students and non-SC/ST students of Education Department High Schools; between the SC/ST students and non-SC/ST students; and between the students of Ashram and the Education Department High Schools.

(b) The non-SC/ST students of Ashram High Schools were having more n-Ach than their SC/ST counterparts.

(c) The non-SC/ST students of Education Department High Schools appeared to have greater magnitude of n-Ach in comparison to the SC/ST students in the same school.

(d) The non-SC/ST students showed superiority over SC/ST students with respect to n-Ach.

(e) The students of Education Department High Schools had significantly higher n-Ach than the students of Ashram High Schools.

(f) No significant difference was noted in the distribution of the n-Ach between the SC/ST students of Ashram High Schools and Education Department High Schools.

DISCUSSION OF RESULTS

The results indicated that the students of Education Department High Schools are from higher socio-economic status than the students of the Ashram High Schools. Similarly the SC/ST students as a whole are from lower socio-economic status than the non-SC/ST students. When the different group combinations are compared it is found that the SC/ST students, irrespective of their school background are from lower socio-economic status than their non-SC/ST counterparts. The comparison of SC/ST students in terms of their socio-economic status across their school typology revealed that the SC/ST students of Ashram High Schools are from lower socio-economic status than the SC/ST students of Education Department High Schools. The obtained findings of the present study seems to be justified on certain grounds. One possible explanation seems to be cultural factor, which need further elaboration. Secondly in the Ashram Schools generally a large number of SC/ST students have been enrolled who belong to disadvantaged group and are socially and economically backward.

In this connection it will be pertinent to refer to some studies. Reissman (1962), Thompson (1962), Goldberg and Tannenbaum (1967) and Witty (1967) reported that low SES, lack of motivation, alienation from the school and the family, language difficulties in learning process and other factors are the important variables for educational retardation and the early drop-out of children coming from the disadvantaged groups in a society. The studies of Desai and Pandor (1974), Rajgopalan (1974), and Kamila (1985) lend support directly to the findings of the study. Their findings indicated significant differences in SES of students belonging to different castes and schools.

Another finding of the study highlights the superiority of Ashram High Schools over Education Department High Schools with regard to school facilities like space, subject teacher, hostel, tutorial arrangement, student-teacher ratio, student-non-teaching personnel ratio and land. May be because of the broad policy guidelines for the Ashram Schools. Ashram School scheme was originally a centrally sponsored scheme, operated by the states. These schools are established as a direct intervention to tackle the socio-economic and geographical inequalities of the tribal population by providing educational opportunities. These schools aim at providing an atmosphere in which the inmates are offered full opportunities to develop their personality. For these reasons special grants and facilities are made available to the Ashram schools. In this connection supporting evidence comes from a study by Kamila (1985).

He found that the Ashram Schools were superior in the facilities like space, teaching aids, subject teacher, hostel, students teacher ratio, student-non-teaching personnel ratio and land than the Education Department High Schools.

Another finding indicates that caste and school had significant effect on the performance of students. The non-SC/ST students performed better than their SC/ST counterparts. Such difference in performance can be attributed to the factors like place of residence, sincerity in studies, home and emotional adjustment, scholastic ability, and parental awareness. Verma (1985) reported that students from higher castes had a more favourbale attitude towards the school, towards the medium of instruction and were from higher socio-economic status than the SC/ST students which might favour them to achieve more. The present finding is supported by Aikara (1980), Kamat (1981), Kamila (1985), Mishra (1989) and Mishra (1998), but contradicts the findings of Agarwal (1981) who reported no caste differences in academic achievement.

The obtained results of effect of school on the performance of students are in consonance with the results of Sujatha and Yeshodhara (1986), and Mishra (1989) who found significant differences between students of Ashram School and Non-Ashram Schools on academic achievement. The rationale for the better performance of the students of Education Department High Schools may be better emotional adjustment, extra coaching, competitive spirit among the students, reinforcement in studies received by the students from their kith and kin, and better cultural consumption.

Results pertaining to the attitude of students indicate that the students belonging to Education Department High Schools have more favourable attitude towards school and curriculum than their Ashram School counterparts. This situation can be explained in terms of organizational climate of the school. It is our common experience that the Education Department High Schools are dominated by the non-SC/ST students whose number is quite large. The findings of the present study together with findings of some other researchers have established it that the non-SC/ST students are high achievers. To achieve high one is supposed to have favourable attitude towards school and curriculum. There is no parallel study (excepting Kamila, 1985) to substantiate the findings. Kamila (1985) found that the non-SC/ST students had favourable attitude towards school, teacher and science teaching than their SC/ST counterparts. Further the non-SC/ST students of Education Department High Schools had favourable attitude towards teacher than their SC/ST counterparts in the same school and the SC/ST students of Ashram Schools had more favourable attitude towards classmates than the SC/ST students of Education Department High Schools. Thus the present finding contradicts the findings of Kamila (1985).

It is also found that the non-SC/ST students taken together have higher level of occupational aspiration than their SC/ST counterparts, and the students of Education Department High Schools as whole have higher level of occupational aspiration than their counterparts in Ashram Schools. Thus caste and school seem to emerge as important determinants of occupational aspiration of students.

The differences in occupational aspiration can be explained on the basis of differences in socio-economic status, differential features of different cultures and lack of acquaintance of students with different types of jobs and financial benefits and socioal prestige attached to them. Incidentally it may be pointed out that Kamila (1985) in his study on Harijan and Tribal Welfare Department High Schools on a sample of 1268 students (i.e. 624 SC/ST students and 644 other caste students) from Orissa reported findings similar to that of present study. Mishra (1989) could not establish any significant differences in occupational aspiration of students across their school and caste. Joshi (1980) observed lower level of occupational aspiration among SC/ST students as against non-SC/ST students.

The results have also shown the effect of caste on the level of educational aspiration. It was found that the SC/ST students had significantly higher level of educational aspiration than their non-SC/ST counterparts. This result seems to be quite surprising because it has been generally observed that the non-SC/ST students aspire more for education than the SC/ST students. This may partly be due to the differences in the type of sample and the areas where from these samples were drawn. The present findings contradict the findings of Mishra (1989) who found no caste effect on educational aspiration of students.

The rationale for difference in educational aspiration may be due to the competitiveness of modern times. With the passage of time and process of modernization the SC/ST students might have started thinking that they must compete with others in the field of education for getting jobs, for feeling secured and thus occupy a position in the society.

The last finding of the study indicated the effect of caste and school on n-Ach. It was found that the non-SC/ST students had more n-Ach than their SC/ST counterparts. The non-SC/ST students of Education Department High Schools had greater magnitude of n-Ach than the SC./ST students in the same school. The non-SC/ST students showed superiority over SC/ST students in n-Ach. Similarly the students of Education Department High Schools had significantly higher n-Ach than the students of Ashram High Schools.

Mcclelland[1] (1961) is of the view that the backward societies have low need for achievement. Singh and Sinha (1982) in their study found that tribal societies were backward in the sense that they had traditional belief, superstition, strong religious attitude, rituals, typical rural norms and customs. These might be the cause of low achievement motivation among backward children.

Singh (1988) stated that Santal parents might find themselves unable to give their children education, emphasizing independence or a training of any high standards of excellence. Actually these children are neither made aware of competitiveness nor they are introduced to any coherent view of success in life. In problem-solving situation, parents do not exhibit their full encouragement, participation and initiative to their children because of their easy-going temperament. Thus these traditional outlooks of the Santal parents may bring up their children in such a way that they negatively affect the achievement motivation of the children (Katz 1970).

The superiority of the students of Education Department High Schools over the students of Ashram High Schools with regard to n-Ach may be due to the degree of environmental challenge being provided by Education Department High Schools. Mcclelland (1961) concluded that environment is not an essential factor for growth of achievement motive, rather degree of environmental challenge can be considered as an essential factor. If the environment supports learning at the critical time, n-Ach will develop to the proper extent.

IMPLICATIONS

The implications of the present piece of research are stated below:

(i) Since the SC/ST students and the students of Ashram Schools were found to be socio-economically poor, more efforts need to be made to increase the socio-economic conditions of the students studying at the secondary level

by way of mid-day meals, uniforms, opportunity cost etc. Also the supervisory authority should see that the stipends are given in time.

Further to suit the economic needs of the community both classroom teaching and crafts taught in the Ashram Schools should have local bias. The lessons should be prepared to suit the varied economic activities of tribals. The practical classes conducted in the attached agricultural farms and vegetable gardens of Ashram Schools should benefit the students.

(ii) The study revealed that the Ashram High Schools were poor in equipments. Special grants may be given to these schools to purchase the required equipment, which will facilitate the teaching learning process.

(iii) The poor performance of the SC./ST students can be tackled with the help of the special remedial classes. The subject teachers should be entrusted with this work.

(iv) The study confirmed the unfavourable attitude of the students of Ashram High Schools towards schools. To develop a positive attitude towards school, the teacher should exemplify himself through different activities of the school.

(v) The students of Ashram High Schools have unfavourable attitude towards curriculum. The school climate programme may be undertaken in this direction.

(vi) Both the SC/ST students and the students of Ashram High Schools were found to have lower level of occupational aspiration. This is not a good sign. Attempts may be made to appoint career masters or counsellors who can provide necessary guidance to the students regarding the various occupations.

(vii) It was found that the non-SC/ST students had lower level of educational aspiration. The reason may be that the non-SC/ST students who had acquired adequate education have failed to secure paid employment. This situation necessitates provision for adequate services in the secondary schools.

(viii) Both the SC/ST students and non-SC/ST students were found to have lower n-Ach. Since the growth of n-Ach is shaped by individual's experiential background, the child rearing practices with special reference to independence training may be given. In this context the role of the family and extension service programmes should be stressed. A child can learn and acquire the motive as a result of the way parents have raised him. The tribal parents may be oriented through non-formal education system to do all these.

SUGGESTIONS

On the basis of the findings of the study the following suggestions can be offered:

(i) This study may be replicated on large samples and in other states so that the generalization of wider nature may be made.

(ii) Case studies may be conducted for acquiring in-depth knowledge into the functions and problems of Ashram High Schools.

(iii) In addition to the present variables other variables such as intelligence, interest, family structure, adjustment pattern, study habit, learning style and creativity etc. may be studied.

(iv) Similar studies may be conducted by controlling the intervening variables like age, sex and socio-economic status.

(v) More objective assessment of n-Ach, attitude, socio-economic status, school facilities, occupational and educational aspirations can be made by using some other type of tests and techniques.

(vi) The present study cannot be comprehensive and final in itself unless subjective to many variations. The sample size can be enlarged comprising stratifications based on age, grade, caste, culture and socio-economic status.

(vii) The findings of the study need further cross validation.

Bibliography

Aiyappan, A.(1948). *Report on the Socio-economic Conditions of the Aboriginal Tribes of the Province of Madras,* New Delhi.: Government of India, 43-44.

Ambasht, N.K. (1970). *A Critical Story of Tribal Education with Special Reference to Ranchi District.* New Delhi: S. Chand & Co.

Ameerjan, M.S. (1987). "Personality and Academic Achievement of SC and ST College Students of Agricultural Sciences: A Comparative Study", *Indian Educational Review.* 22 (2).

Ananda, G. (1994). *Ashram Schools in Andhra Pradesh,* New Delhi: Common Wealth Publishers.

Apte, J.S. (1960). "Talwada Ashram School—An Experiment in Tribal Education", *Vanyajati,* VIII (3).

Arun, N.S. (1981). A Study of the Factors Influencing the Achievement of ST. VII students belonging to SCs and STs whose medium of instruction is Kannada", In M.B. Buch (1987), *Third Survey of Research in Education,* New Delhi: N.C.E.R.T.

Banarjee, S.K. (1962) Some Differential Effects on Primary Education of the Tribal Students of West Bengal; *Bulletin of the Cultural Research Institute,* Calcutta, 1(2), 46-53.

Bapat, N.V. (1961). "Tribal Education—A Problem", *Vanyajati,* IX(1), 37-39.

Basu, M.N. (1958). "The Role of Anthropology in the Education of Aborigines in India", *Adivasi,* III (2), 1-8.

Basu, M.N. (1961). "Suggestions for the Educational Plan of Aboriginal People of India", *Vanyajati,* IX (3), 123-126.

Bernstein,B. (1962). Linguistic Codes, Hestation Phenomena and Intelligence. *Language and Speech,* 5, 31-46.

Best, J.W. (1977). *Research in Education*. New Delhi: Prentice-Hall of India. Pvt. Ltd.

Bhuriya, M. (1979). *Folk Songs of the Bhils*. Indore: Mahipal Publication.

Bose, S.A. (1963). Sociological Study of Adolescent Tribal Children of West Himalayan Region for Purpose of National Integration Participation, Calcutta, University of Calcutta, Ph.D. Thesis. Calcutta University.

Bruner, J.S. (1975). Poverty and Childhood, (*Oxford Review of Education*), Vol-I.

Chttopadhyay, K.D. (1978). *Tribalism in India*. New Delhi: Vikas Publishing House.

Coleman, J.S. (1966). *Equality of Educational Opportunity*. Washington D.C., U.S. Government Printing Office, 34.

Cronbach, L.J. (1963). *Essentials of Psychological Testing*. New York: Harper and Row.

Dasgupta, N.K. (1964). "Problems of Tribal Education and the Santals". New Delhi: *Bharatiya Adimajati Sevak Sangh*, 39.

Dave, P.C. (1954). "Report on Ashram Schools, Sevashrams and Training Cadres in Orissa State" *Vanyajati II* (63).

Davis, A. (1948). *Social Class Influences Upon Learning*. Cambridge: Harvard University Press, 29.

Desai,I.P. (1974). *A Profile of Education Among the STs of Gujarat*. Surat: Centre for Regional Development Studies.

Deutsch, C.P. (1964). Auditory Discrimination and Learning: Social Factors, *Merril-Palmer Quarterly*, 10(3), 277-296.

Deutsch, C.P. (1965). "Education for Disadvantaged Groups" *Review of Educational Research*, XX (2).

Deutsch, M. (1963). The Disadvantaged Child and the Learning Process: Some Social, Psychological and Developmental Considerations, *Education in Depressed Areas*, New York: Teachers College, Columbia University, 196

Deutsch, M. (1965). The Role of Social Class in Language Development and Cognition, *American Journal of Orthopsychiatry*, 35, 78-88.

Dimaggio, P. (1982). "Cultural Capital and School Success: The Impact of Status Culture Participation on the Grades of U.S. High School Students". *American Sociological Review*, 47.

Dube, B.K. & Bahadur, F. (1966). *A Study of the Tribal People and Tribal Areas of Madhya Pradesh*, Bhopal: Tribal Research and Development Institute, 6, N.2. Dec.

Dubey, S.M. (1974). *Study of Scheduled Caste and Scheduled Tribe College Students in Assam*: Delhi, Department of Sociology, Delhi University.

Elwin, V. (1963). *A New Deal of Tribal India*, New Delhi: Government of India, Ministry of Home Affairs.

Farley, R.(1977). "Trends in Racial Inequalities: Have the Gains of the 1960s Disappeared in the 1970s?" *American Sociological Review*, 42, 189-207.

Feldhuson, J.F. and Klausmeir, J.H. (1962). Anxiety, Intelligence and Achievement in Children of Low, and Average Intelligence, *Child Development*, 33, 403-409.

Garrett, H.E. (1979). *Statistics in Psychology and Education*. Bombay: Vakils, Feffer and Simons Ltd.

George, E.I. (1975). *Educational Problems of Scheduled Caste and Scheduled Tribe College Students in Kerala*. Trivandrum, Department of Psychology, Kerala University.

Gill, R.T. (1965). *Economic Development: Past and Present*. New Delhi: Prentice Hall of India Pvt. Ltd.

Gokulnathan, P.P. (1972). "A Study of Achievement Related Motivation and Educational Achievement Among Secondary School Pupils". Ph.D. Education, Dibrugarh University.

Goode, C.V., Barr, A.S. and Scates, D.E. (1941). *Methodology of Educational Research*. New York: Appleton Century Crofts, Inc.

Green, R.L. and Farquhar, W.W. (1965). Negro Academic Motivation and Scholastic Achievement, *Journal of Educational Psychology* 56, 241-243.

Grigson, W.V. (1947). *Challenge of Backwardness*, Hyderabad: Government Press.

Havighurst, R.J. (1964). *The Public Schools of Chicago*. Chicago: The Board of Education of the City of Chicago.

Haywood, H.C. (1967). "Experiential Factors in Intellectual Development: The Concept of Dynamic Intelligence". In Zubin, J, and Jervis, G. *Psychology of Mental Development*, New York: Grure and Stratton, 67.

Heda, H.C. (1965). Tribal Education: Integration Aspect Rashtra Sanatas, A Novel Scheme, Souvenir, Hyderabad: Andhra Pradesh Adimjati Sevak Sangh.

Herzog, E and Lewis, H. (1971). Children in Poor Families: Myths and Realities. In S. Chess and A. Thomson, eds. *Annual Progress in Child Psychiatry and Child Development,* New York: Bruner/Mazel, 307-322.

Hillway, T. (1956). *Introduction to Research Boston*: Hughton Mifflin.

John, V.P. and Goldstein, L.S. (1964). The Social Context of Language Acquisition, *Merril-palmer Quarterly*, 10, 265-275.

Jones, J.A. (1963). Social Class: Educational Attitudes, and Participation. In H.Passow (1967) *Education in Depressed Areas*, New York: Teacher College Press, Columbia University, 119-129.

Joshi, S.D. (1980). Educational Problems of SCs and STs of Baroda District. In M.B. Buch (1987), *Third Survey of Research in Education*, New Delhi: N.C.E.R.T.

Kagan, J. (1965). Reflection-impulsivity and Reading Ability in Primary Grade Children. *Child Development*, 36(3), 609-628.

Kamat, V.C. (1981). "A Comparative Study of the Self-perception of Backward Class and Non-backward Class Students and their Socio-economic Status, Vocational and Educational Aspiration, Educational Achievement and School Environment". In M.B. Buch, (1987), *Third Survey of Research in Education.* New Delhi: NCERT.

Kamila, B.B. (1985). An Evaluative Study of HTW Department High Schools in Orissa in Respect of Student Achievement. Ph.D. Education, Visva Bharati.

Katz, I. (1970). "A New Approach to the Study of School Motivation in Minority Group Children", In V.I. Aleen (Ed) (1975), *Psychological Factors in Poverty*, New York: Academic Press.

Kaul, S.K. (1967). "Existing Facilities, Coverage, Wastage, Stagnation and Utilization of Financial Assistance in Respect of Tribal

Education", *Tribal Education in India*. Report of the National Seminar, New Delhi: NCERT, 67-76.

Khurana, G.K. (1978). Approach to Education of Scheduled Tribes, *The Education Quarterly*, XXX(I).

Kohn, M.L. (1959). "Social Class and Parental Values, *American Journal of Sociology*, 64-(4).

Korchhoff, A.C. (1959). Anomic and Achievement Motivation: A Study of Personality Development Within Cultural Disorganization, *Social Forces*, 37, 196-202.

Labov, W. *et al.* (1968). *A Study of the Non-standard English of Negro and Puertorican Speakers in New York City*, 2 Vols. New York: Columbia University (Mimeographed).

Leshan, I.L. (1952). Time Orientation and Social Class. *Journal of Abnormal and Social Psychology* 48, 582-592.

Liebert, R.M. *et al.* (1979). *"Developmental Psychology,* New Delhi: Prentice Hall of India Pvt. Ltd.

Mead, M.(1953). *Cultural Patterns and Technical Change*. Paris: UNESCO.

Mehta, B.M. (1976). "The Problems of Aborigines" *The Indian Journal of Social Work*, X (2), 88-92.

Mehta, P.H., Bhatnagar, A. and Jain, V.K. (1993). *Psycho-Educational Studies of Tribal Students of Meghalaya*. N. Delhi: NCERT.

Miller, J.O. and Mumbauer, C. (1967). *Intellectual Functioning, Learning Performance and Cognitive Style in Advantaged and Disadvantaged Pre-school Children*. Unpublished Manuscript, George Peaboy College for Teachers.

Mishra, A. (1977) *Role of Education in Tribal Education*, New Delhi: Government of India, Ministry of Home Affairs, Occasional Paper on Tribal Development.

Mishra, B.B. (1989). "Personality Patterns, Occupational and Educational Aspirations and Academic Achievement of SC and ST Students Studying in Ashram Schools of Orissa", Ph.D. Education, Kurukshetra University.

Mishra, B.C.(1996), *Education of Tribal Children*. New Delhi: Discovery Publishing House.

Mishra, B.C. (1998) "A Comparative Study of the Personality Patterns and Academic Achievement of SC and ST Students and Non-SC/ST Students Studying in Ashram Schools and Non Ashram Schools in Orissa". Project Report Submitted to the ERIC, New Delhi: N.C.E.R.T.

Mouly, G.J. (1963). *The Science of Educational Research*. New Delhi: Eurasia Publishing House Pvt. Ltd.

Murray, H.A. (1938). *Exploration in Personality*. New York: Oxford University Press.

Naik, T.B. (1969). Impact of Education on the Bhils: Culture Change in Tribal, New Delhi: Research Programme Committee, Planning Commission.

Narain, V. (1996). "Achievement Motivation in Tribal and Non-tribal Women", *Indian Educational Review*, 31 (2), 92-97.

Nayar, P.K.B. (1975). *The SCs and STs in Kerala*. Trivandrum: Kerala University. Department of Sociology.

Panda, B.N. (1986). "*Personality Adjustment, Mental Health and Acculturation Among Saora Tribals*", Doctoral Dissertation, Education, Kurukshetra University.

Panda, S.K. and Panigrahi, S.C.(1984). "Personality Patterns of Tribal and Non-tribal Tenth Graders: A Cross-cultural Study", *Journal of Educational Research and Extension*, 20 (4).

Parvathamma, C. (1974). *The Study of SC and ST College Students in Karnataka State*. Mysore: Department of Post-graduate Studies and Research, University of Mysore.

Patel, D. (1987). "Academic Achievement in Relation to Cognitive and Personality Differentials of Socially Disadvantaged and Advantaged Secondary School Children of Orissa. In M.B. Buch (1991). Ed. *Fourth Survey of Research in Education*, New Delhi: N.C.E.R.T.

Pattanaik, N.(1957). "An Appraisal of Ashram School Education" Report of the Fourth Conference for Tribes and Tribals (Scheduled) Areas, New Delhi: Bharatiya Adimjati Sevak Sangh.

Rajgopalan, C. (1974). *Educational Progress and Problem of Scheduled Caste and Scheduled Tribe Students in Karnataka*, Department of Sociology, Bangalore University.

Ramana, G.V. (1990). "Problems of Education Among the Tribal Communities of Andhra Pradesh", A Case Study of Ashram Schools, Ph.D. Diss, Sri Venkateswara University, Tirupati.

Rao, V.K.R.V. (1966). *Education and Human Resources Development*. New Delhi: Allied Publishers.

Rath, R. (1972). "*Cognitive Growth and Class-room Learning of Culturally Deprived Children in Primary Schools*", Papers Presented at the East West Center for Cross Cultural Studies. Honolulu.

Rath, R. (1974b). "*Teaching Learning Problems of the Disadvantaged Tribal Children*"; Presidential Address at the Twelfth Annual Conference of Indian Academy of Applied Psychology. U.U.

Rath, R. (1976). "Problems of Equalization of Educational Opportunities for the Tribal Children, *Indian Educational Review*, IX (2)

Rathnaiah, E.V. (1977). *Structural Constraints of Tribal Education: A Regional Study*. New Delhi: Sterling Publishers.

Riessman, F. (1962). *The Culturally Deprived Child*. New York: Harper and Row, 97.

Robinson, W.P. (1965). "The Elaborated Code in Working Class Language", *Language and Speech*, 8, 243-252.

Rosen, B.C. and Andrade, R.D. (1959). The Psychological Origins of Achievement Motivation, *Sociometry*, 22, 185-218.

Rosenberg, M. (1965). *Society and the Adolescent Self-image*. Princeton: Princeton University Press.

Sachidananda (1964). "Tribal Education in India" Vanyajati Bhartiya Adimjati Sevak Sangh, VII(I).

Sachidananda (1967). *Socio-economic Aspect of Tribal Education*, in Report of the National Seminar on Tribal Education in India, New Delhi; N.C.E.R.T.

Sachidananda (1974). *Education Among the SCs and STs in Bihar School Students*, Patna: A.N. Sinha Institute of Social Studies.

Shah B.V. and Thaker, T.D. (1974). *Educational Problems of SC and ST Students in Gujarat*. Department of Sociology S.P. University, Gujarat.

Shah, V.P. and Patel, T(1985). *Social Context of Tribal Education*, New Delhi: Concept Publishing Co.

Sharma, D.P. (1977). "Personality Syndromes of Scheduled Caste and Non Scheduled Caste Pupil Teachers", Unpublished M.Ed Dissertation, Meerut University.

Sharma, K.R. (1977). "Specific Problems of Tribal Schools", *Education Quarterly*, XXVIII (2), 30-33.

Sharma, K.R. (1991). *Educational Life Style of Tribal Students*. New Delhi: Classical Publishing Co.

Singh, L.B. (1980). "A Comparative Study of Academic Achievement of Santal and Non-santal Undergraduate Students of Santal Praganas District of Bihar". *Journal of Educational Research and Extension*, 16 (3).

Singh, T. (1981). "Achievement of Tribal Students in Relation to their Intelligence, Motivation and Personality. In M.B. Buch (1987) *Third Survey of Research in Education*, New Delhi: NCERT.

Singh, L.B.(1988). *Santal Youth: An Unseen Talent*: New Delhi: Wisdom Publication.

Singh, N.K. (1975). "Educational Problems of the SC and ST School Students in Rajasthan", Department of Soc, Raj.Univ. (ICSSR Financed).

Srivastava, L.R.N. (1967). An *Annotated Bibliography on Tribal Education in India*, New Delhi: N.C.E.R.T.

Srivastava, L.R.N. (ed) (1967). *Tribal Education in India* Report of the National Seminar on Tribal Education in India, New Delhi, N.C.E.R.T.

Srivastava, L.R.N. *et al.* (1971a). *An Integrated and Comparative Study of a Selected Tribal Community Living in Contiguous Areas*, New Delhi: N.C.E.R.T

Srivastava, L.R.N. (1971a), *Identification of Educational Problems of the Saora of Orissa*, New Delhi:N.C.E.R.T.

Srivastava, P. (1986). "A Socio-psychological Study of Stagnates Among Tribal and Non-tribal Students of Class VIII" In M.B. Buch (1991), *Fourth Survey of Research in Education*, New Delhi; N.C.E.R.T.

Srivastava, P. (1986). "A Socio-psychological Study of Stagnates Among Tribal and Non-tribal Students of Class VIII" In M.B. Buch (1991), *Fourth Survey of Research in Education*, New Delhi: N.C.E.R.T.

Strauss, M.A. (1962). "Deferred Gratification, Social Class and the Achievement Syndrome", *American Sociological Review*, 27.

Sujata, B.N. and Yeshodhara, K.A. (1986). "A Comparative Study of Some Educational Variables of SC/ST Students", In M.B. Buch (1991), *Fourth Survey of Research in Education*, New Delhi: N.C.E.R.T.

Sujatha, K. (1987) "Ashram Schools for Tribal Children" *New Frontiers in Education*, XVII (40).

Sujatha, K. (1987). *Education of the Forgotten Children of the Forests: A Study of Yenadi Tribe.* New Delhi; Konark Publishers Pvt. Ltd.

Taydor, G. and Ayers, N (1969). Born and Bred Unequal, London: Longman.

Thompson, C., H., (1962). "Problems in Achievement of Adequate Educational Opportunity. In Clift, Vigil A. (E.d) *Negro Education in America, Its Adequacy, Problems and Needs*, New York: Harper and Row.

Uzgiris, I.C. (1968). *Socio-cultural Factors in Cognitive Development.* Paper Presented at the Peabody NIMH Conference on Socio-Cultural Aspects of Mental Retardation, Tennessee: Nashville, June.

Verma, M. (1985). "Factors Affecting Academic Achievement; A Cross-cultural Study of Tribal and Non-tribal Students at Junior High School Level in U.P." Ph.D. Education. Avadh University.

Verma, S.C. (1978). *The Bhil Kills*. Delhi: Kunj Publishing House.

Vyas, A.N. (1958). "Ten Years Progress of Ashram Education in Orissa", *Vanyajati*, VI(4), 157.

Wax, Murry L., Dumant, R.V. Jr. and Wax Rassalie, R. (1964). *Formal Education in an Indian Community*", Kalamazoo, Mich: Society for the Study of Social Problems.

Witty, Paul, A.(ed) (1967). *The Educationally Retarded and Disadvantaged*; Chicago, Illinois; National Society for the Study of Education.

Wylie, R.C. (1963). Children's Estimates of their School Work Ability as a Function of Sex, Race and Socio-economic Level, *Journal of Personality*, 31, 203-224.

Index